MW01441540

JUSTICE SERVED:
HOW I REPRESENTED MYSELF
TO VICTORY

"You never know how strong you are until being strong is the only choice you have."

OWENS-COLLINS ENTERPRISES, LLC

The author has tried to recreate events, locations, and conversations from her memories of them. She may also have changed some identifying characteristics and details such as physical attributes, occupations, and places of residence. This book is not intended as a substitute for the legal advice of lawyers or attorneys. The reader should consult a lawyer or attorney regularly in any matters relating to his/her legal disputes.

Copyright © 2023 by Dr. Sheila Owens-Collins

All rights reserved. No part of this book may be reproduced or transmitted in any form or by any means, electronic or mechanical, including photocopying, recording, or any information storage and retrieval system, without permission in writing from the author.

ISBN: 979-8-9897974-2-4 – Hardcover
ISBN: 979-8-9897974-1-7 – Paperback
eISBN: 979-8-9897974-0-0 – KDP

These ISBNs are the property of Dr. Sheila Owens Collins for the express purpose of sales and distribution of this title. The content of this book is the property of the copyright holder only.

To my beloved mother - Mrs. Hattie Lester Balfour Owens and her life partner Dr. Emiel Wade Owens -
You taught me to handle adversity with courage, a spirit of forgiveness, compassion, faith in God, and grace.
Thank you! I'm eternally grateful.
With all my love always!

Your daughter,
Sheila

PRELUDE

In the world of medicine, where I have spent my life as a dedicated pediatrician, you are taught to be prepared for anything. Yet, nothing could have prepared me for the whirlwind of legal battles that awaited me when I was unexpectedly thrust into the role of fighting the guardianship of my beloved mother, followed by the will contest, and the battle that is still ongoing over the execution of my mother's will.

When my mother passed away, my world was further shaken by the contentious dispute over her will. My siblings, driven by greed, financial desperation, jealousy of me and my two sons, resentment, and blame toward our parents for how their lives turned out, contested the document that clearly outlined her final wishes. It was not a problem that the will divided the estate equally between the four siblings, the problem was that I was the 1st Executor, my son was the 2nd Executor, and they were unnamed. This led us to a probate judge who, from my perspective, showed a clear bias throughout the guardianship fee contest trial, as well as the will contest trial.

Despite the evident hostilities, bad faith, and pettiness of the disgruntled family members contesting the will, the judge ruled to admit the will, which named me as the executor. However, he disqualified me from the role, citing family discord as the reason. The impact of the judge's conduct and biased decisions culminated in this final decision in the will contest trial - a ruling that was a punch to the gut, undermining the trust placed in me by my late mother and robbing me of the chance to honor her wishes.

But I wasn't ready to back down. Drawing on the same tenacity that fueled my medical career, I decided to fight back. I took the bold step of suing the judge in federal court. Subsequently, I filed a motion for his recusal, a move that proved successful and brought about a turning point in my legal journey. The case was reassigned to a new judge, who, in stark contrast to his predecessor, ruled in favor of honoring the original will. This decision reinstated the estate back to our family and recognized my son as the second rightful executor, as per my mother's intentions.

This book charts my tumultuous journey, offering an insight into a system that both challenged and changed me. It is a story of resistance and resilience, of standing up for justice, and ultimately, of a victory that honored my mother's last wishes. At the end of every chapter, I share the lessons that I learned and the recommended action steps to reach your goals.

DISCLAIMER

The information provided in this book does not, and is not intended to, constitute legal advice; instead, all information, content, and materials available in this book are for general informational purposes only. Information in this book may not constitute the most up-to-date legal or other information. Readers of this book should contact their attorney to obtain advice with respect to any particular legal matter. No reader should act or refrain from acting based on information in this book without first seeking legal advice from counsel in the relevant jurisdiction. Only your individual attorney can provide assurances that the information contained herein – and your interpretation of it – is applicable or appropriate to your situation. The views expressed in this book are those of the author. Any references made to specific individuals, including attorneys, judges, and family members, should be interpreted within the context of my personal narrative. All liability with respect to actions taken or not taken based on the contents of this book are hereby expressly disclaimed. The content in this book is provided "as is"; no representations are made that the content is error-free.

TABLE OF CONTENTS

CHAPTER 1. INTRODUCTION 1
Overview of My Parents' Estate 2
Probate Court Issues and Family Dynamics 4
Sinister Plot: Unleashing a Covetous Conspiracy 5
    Post-Judgment Proceedings 12
    Summary of the Argument 14
Lessons Learned! 17
Actionable Steps 19

CHAPTER 2. THE PROBATE SYSTEM UNVEILED 21
The Role of the Judge in Estate and Trust Cases 24
Common Issues and Controversies Within the Probate System 28
Lessons Learned! 33
Actionable Steps 34

CHAPTER 3. THE BATTLE CONTINUES 37
Account of the Initial Court Proceedings 37
Outcomes Related to National Institute of Health Stroke Scale (NIHSS) Score at Admission 41
Preparing For a Will Contest Trial 45
Notes from the Bench Trial 52
The Verdict and My Decision to Sue the Judge 54
Lessons Learned! 58

ix

Actionable Steps 61

CHAPTER 4. PREPARING TO WAGE WAR 63

Overview of the Legal Research Conducted 66

Legal Research on "How to Sue a Judge?" 74

How to Disqualify a Judge for Bias 76

The Importance of Understanding Legal Jargon and Court Procedures 78

Lessons Learned! 81

Actionable Steps 83

CHAPTER 5. FILING THE LAWSUIT 85

The Step-by-Step Guide that I Followed: 85

    Step 1: 85

    Step 2: 87

    Step 3: 88

Template for Filing a Lawsuit in Federal Court 99

Template for Completing the Complaint Section 102

Initial Reactions and Responses 104

Lessons Learned! 106

Actionable Steps 106

CHAPTER 6. MOTION FOR RECUSAL 109

Explanation of What a Motion for Recusal Is 109

Case Timeline 113

This Is How I Made My Case 114

CHAPTER 7. THE AFTERMATH 131

    Lessons Learned! 136

    Actionable Steps 138

CHAPTER 8. REGAINING THE ESTATE AND TRUST 139

    Step-By-Step Account of How the Estate and Trust Were Regained .. 139

    Lessons Learned! 147

    Actionable Steps 148

CHAPTER 9. REFLECTIONS AND DISCUSSION OF LESSONS LEARNED 151

    Unholy Alliances 156

    Some Potential Solutions 158

    Mental Health Issues 159

    My Advice to Others Who May Find Themselves in a Similar Situation 163

CHAPTER 10. CONCLUSION AND CALL TO ACTION 167

    Call to Action: Reforming the Guardianship and Probate System 168

        Call to Action 169

DEFINITIONS, ROLES, AND RESPONSIBILITIES 173

REFERENCES 181

CHAPTER 1. INTRODUCTION

As the firstborn child in my family, I was naturally imbued with many of the qualities typically ascribed to those who lead the sibling line. High-achieving, motivated, and always eager to make my parents proud, I took on the world with tenacity and determination. My parents, both educators and valedictorians of their respective high school classes, instilled in me the value of education from a young age. Their shared love story began at Prairie View A&M University, where they met, fell in love, and tied the knot, all while on scholarships earned through their hard work and dedication.

Growing up, the importance of education was not just emphasized, it was celebrated. Accepting this challenge, I graduated third in my high school class, earned a regent's scholarship to the University of California, San Diego (UCSD), and later pursued a career in medicine. The joy and pride in my parents' eyes were my biggest rewards. Our bond remained unshaken and strong throughout the years, a closeness that was seamlessly transferred to my two sons. The beginning of this journey is a story of familial love, educational pursuit, and the enduring values passed down through generations.

Overview of My Parents' Estate

At the heart of my parents' estate is a stunningly unique, 6,000-square-foot house that was thoughtfully designed and built by my father in 1972. This architectural marvel features five bedrooms, seven bathrooms, a separate living room adjoined to the master bedroom, a well-stocked library, and a dynamic game room. The property even boasts distinct boy and girl changing rooms, a charming detail that speaks to my father's meticulous planning.

Anchored close to the medical center, this home enjoys an enviable location in Houston. It offers proximity to everything significant in the city, making it not just a beautiful residence but also a strategically placed asset. Initially built for $62,000, the house has appreciated over the years and is currently valued at an impressive $1.38 million.

Introduction

But my father's vision didn't stop with our family home. In a move that was unusually forward-thinking for his generation, he also constructed two student housing complexes in Prairie View. These properties were intended to supplement our family income and provide extra funds for his retirement. His foresight and dedication to providing for his family have left an enduring legacy that continues to benefit us today.

The period between my father's death and my mother's passing spanned over eleven long years. During this time, we navigated the complexities of their estate, which included assets both shared and separate. My father, ever the planner, had set up a Revocable Trust during his lifetime. The deed to our family home, his pride and joy, was the sole property contained within this trust. When my mother passed away, she left behind a will that clearly outlined her wishes regarding the execution of her estate. I was named as the 1st Executor, a role that reflected the trust and confidence she placed in me. My son was designated as the 2nd Executor, followed by her nephew who was listed as the 3rd Executor.

Probate Court Issues and Family Dynamics

Navigating through the probate court can present numerous challenges, not least of which are those stemming from familial conflicts and personal issues. As outlined in multiple sources, common problems can include misunderstandings over inheritance, conflicts over the decedent's will, beneficiaries not being properly named, and ambiguous wording in the will.

https://www.estateandprobatelawyer.com

High-risk factors for probate litigation often include sibling rivalry and dysfunctional families. https://www.justia.com/

In my situation, these challenges were magnified by the personal struggles of my siblings. My sister, with a history of illicit drug use, and my youngest brother, who grappled with alcohol issues, were both desperate for cash. Added to this mix was my sister's childless daughter in her 40s, who had previously asked my mother for $29,000 for in vitro fertilization—a request that my mother wisely denied. Their desperation reached a point where they wanted my mother moved out of her house and into a nursing home, with the ulterior motive of selling the house for the cash they so urgently needed. The arrival of Hurricane Harvey provided them with a perfect opportunity to execute this plan, marking the first step in what can only be described as an evil, greedy scheme.

After Hurricane Harvey, amidst the chaos and family tensions, my siblings and niece swiftly took action and made the probate court a battleground for our family. The following actions were taken, and in such rapid sequence and coordination with the court-appointed attorneys that it took my breath away.

Sinister Plot: Unleashing a Covetous Conspiracy

On September 15, 2017, strapped for cash, my sister and her daughter took my mother to an attorney and misled her into signing a new Power of Attorney that added the granddaughter's name to it. They then went to all of her banks and collected bank statements. I found out about it 24 hours later. When I explained to my mother what had happened, she was very hurt and angry about how she had been betrayed and insisted that I get her granddaughter off of the POA, which I did on September 17, 2017. At the same time, I made arrangements for my mother to relocate to an assisted living apartment while her house was being repaired from damage by Hurricane Harvey.

Justice Served: How I Represented Myself to Victory

On September 18, 2017, they went to my mother's apartment and started screaming and yelling at her so loudly and relentlessly that the apartment security came and escorted them off the property. Continuing their retaliation, they then went to Adult Protective Services and made a slew of false allegations about me followed by a visit to the guardianship court to proclaim that my mother was incapacitated, I was exploiting her, and my niece wanted to be appointed her guardian. Both of them had criminal records, but my niece's record was less severe so she was nominated by her mother and uncle to apply for my mother's guardianship. In addition, my sister had made two prior false complaints against me over the prior ten years to Child Protective Services and Adult Protective Services and was warned that another false complaint would be met with charges against her from APS as well as from me.

My niece and sister presented my mother to court-appointed attorneys who exhibited predatory behaviors on a silver platter. They told them that my mother needed to be in guardianship because she was incapacitated and by the way, she had a house

Introduction

that was worth $1M. The salivation began. The courts ignored the red flag that 72 hours prior to declaring my mother incapacitated, when they coerced her into signing a POA, there were no concerns about incapacity. The judge even remarked that "she sees this all the time"! They were clearly retaliating because she took the granddaughter/niece off the POA that they misled her into signing.

There was a brief hearing, during which my mother was permitted to approach the bench. She pleaded with the judge to not put her in guardianship, stated that she absolutely did not want my sister or her daughter involved in her affairs, that I had always taken care of her, and she did not want our relationship interrupted. The hearing was short and at the end, my mother was placed in temporary guardianship. I felt that the hearing was not fairly concluded based on its merits and there was a lack of adequate exploration of less restrictive alternatives. The temporary guardianship was supposed to last for 60 days. Immediately after the hearing, the judge appointed a temporary guardian (TG), attorney ad litem (AAL), and guardian ad litem (GAL).

Justice Served: How I Represented Myself to Victory

A very long year began, which was nothing short of hell for my mother. Starting with the presiding judge to the court-appointed attorney, court-appointed guardian ad litem, and court-appointed temporary guardian, it felt like all efforts were spent maligning my character, isolating and medically neglecting my mother, and deceptively labeling her as incapacitated despite evidence and witnesses that would testify otherwise. They were never given a day in court, neither was I and most importantly, neither was my mother.

At the end of the year, there were no hearings or signs of any changes to the status quo. My siblings, niece, and the attorneys were working on finding a permanent guardian for my mother. My mother realized that she was not getting out of her situation and told me that she would rather die than stay in it. And so, she did.

The first hearing after my mother's death was to contest the fees that the attorneys were filing. This was our first meeting with the judge who would later be recused. We entered the hearing with

Introduction

full knowledge of how a "guardianship" should work and the rights of the "ward." In my opinion, the guardianship was fraudulently set up, my mother's rights were violated, and none of the court-appointed attorneys performed their duty to the ethical and legal standards associated with their position.

At that time, I was still represented by attorneys. They wisely recommended that I bring an appellate lawyer to the proceedings in anticipation that I would have to file an appeal. I also had an expert witness to testify about the legal obligations of the temporary guardian, guardian ad litem, and attorney ad litem, their deficiencies in performing their duties, and the excessive and unreasonable fees that were charged to my mother's estate.

The process and outcome of the hearing formed the basis for my appeal, and can be summarized as follows:

The expert witness testified to her extensive experience and qualifications in the area of Texas guardianship law. (4/29/19.) Through the voluminous objections of the attorney the temporary guardian hired to represent her, the Expert testified to the duties of an attorney ad litem (AAL), guardian ad litem (GAL), and temporary guardian (TG). She detailed the deficiencies in the performance of the appointees in this case and that they were not entitled to the fees claimed. The common element was the appointees' failure to take any actions to carry out the desire of my mother to avoid guardianship. None had undertaken any investigation of the claim of financial mismanagement my niece made against me. Because that was the basis of the original application, had they done so, the guardianship could have been resolved early on. She also addressed the fee applications. With regard to the application of the TG, the court required her to identify each challenged item in the 36-page billing records. The hearing concluded without a ruling.

The day after the hearing, the guardian ad litem (GAL) filed an application with the court for additional fees of $4,462.50 which covered a three-month period prior to the hearing. The TG attorney filed an application for payment of $1,764.00, and the TG filed an application for an additional $4,200.00 in fees to be paid to her attorney for representing her.

Introduction

The Trial Court awarded $90,000 in fees without any express ruling on my objections to the fee requests. The trial court (judge) began signing orders awarding fees on May 3, 2019. He signed orders awarding fees of $15,000.00 to the attorney ad litem (AAL), $13,196.38 to the guardian ad litem (GAL), and $53,468.00 to the temporary guardian (TG). The court clerk did not send notice of these orders to the parties in accordance with Rule 306a.[1] On May 28, 2019, the TG filed a second amended final account. The document did not address many of the deficiencies identified by the expert witness but did remove my mother's home from the inventory, agreeing that ownership had been transferred to a trust before the death of my father. Significantly, the document was not signed.

---

[1] Rule 306a (Tx. Rules of Civ. P) pertains to the periods that run from the signing of judgment. The rule states that the date of judgment or order is signed as shown on record shall determine the beginning of these periods. In simpler terms, the court loses jurisdiction in 30 days from the date the order is signed.

Parties involved have only this time to file all necessary documents. It's essential to note that judges, attorneys, and clerks are directed to use their best efforts to ensure all judgments, decisions, and orders of any kind are reduced to writing and signed. This rule is critical in ensuring the timely processing of court decisions and maintaining the integrity of the legal processes.

Moving further, on May 29, 2019, the trial court (judge) signed six more orders. They awarded additional fees to the TG's attorney, the GAL, and the AAL. Even though the final account filed by the TG was not signed, the trial court signed an order approving the final account and all of the fees requested. It signed a separate order dropping the case from the court's docket. Again, the clerk did not give notice of these orders, including the final order. In May 2019, the court ordered payment of $93,410.38 from my mother's estate for a guardianship proceeding she opposed.

Post-Judgment Proceedings

I eventually learned of the orders, filed a motion to extend post-judgment deadlines under Rule 306a, and motioned for a new trial on June 28, 2019. I gave notice of appeal on July 12, 2019. The trial court conducted a hearing on post-judgment motions on September 17, 2019. It found I did not get timely notice of some of the orders and the extended deadlines of Rule 306a applied in that case. The court denied my motion for a new trial. It also

Introduction

refused to make requested findings of fact and conclusions of law[2]. Two requests were made with no response.

---

[2] Findings of Fact and Conclusions of Law are two critical aspects of the decision-making process in a court case.

Findings of Fact
These are the essential facts that a judge or jury determines based on the evidence presented in the case. They include information about what happened, who was involved, when and where it occurred, and other relevant details.

For example, if a car accident case is being tried, the findings of fact might include details such as the date and time of the accident, the weather conditions at the time, the actions of the drivers involved, and the resulting damages.

Conclusions of Law
Once the facts have been determined, the judge (or occasionally the jury) applies the relevant legal principles to those facts to reach the Conclusions of Law. These conclusions determine the outcome of the case. The judge uses the applicable law, such as statutes, regulations, and case law, to interpret the facts and decide who is legally responsible.

For example, in the car accident case mentioned earlier, the judge might apply laws relating to negligence to the facts to conclude whether one driver was legally at fault for the accident.

It's important to note that Findings of Fact and Conclusions of Law must be clearly distinguished in the court's final judgment. This distinction is crucial because appellate courts review these two areas differently: they give deference to the lower court's Findings of Fact (unless they're clearly erroneous), but they review the Conclusions of Law de novo, meaning they decide them anew without any deference to the lower court's decision.

Summary of the Argument

The Texas Estates Code permits a court to appoint attorneys and others to fulfill specific statutorily defined roles in a guardianship proceeding. Those roles are designed to protect the rights of proposed wards, including the right to avoid being subject to the burden of living under the control of a guardian if they object to guardianship or the applicant for guardianship does not meet their requirements. If those appointed by a court do not fulfill their duties, not only are the rights of proposed wards burdened by an unnecessary guardianship, but their estate is burdened by the cost of a superfluous guardianship service too.

The volume of guardianship proceedings in Harris County not only supports specialized probate courts, it also supports attorneys with practices that derive significant funds from court appointments in various roles in guardianship proceedings. This case illustrates the failure of judicial supervision to ensure that the attorneys fulfill their statutory duties, including diligently investigating

Introduction

and seeking to carry out a client's desire to avoid guardianship. The record here is clear that the proposed ward opposed guardianship. She understood the need for assistance and proposed statutorily recognized alternatives to guardianship.

Nevertheless, multiple court appointees took no action to oppose the application or conduct any investigation into the basis for the allegation. Several affirmatively stated they had no duty to do so. The record reflects the response of the court's appointees when their performance is questioned. The record affirmatively reflects personal attacks by court-appointed attorneys, describing a party (me) opposing guardianship in derogatory terms and my attorney as "delusional" in statements to the court and court filings. The record reflected only a few admonitions by the trial court (judge) to act with civility.

I as an Appellant challenged the award of approximately $90,000.00 of my mother's estate to court appointees for a temporary guardianship that lasted just over a year. The temporary guardianship was only supposed to last 60 days. We did not see the first presiding judge over the temporary guardianship until nine months later when she denied my request for a hearing and ordered us to seek mediation.

This was the first encounter with this judge since my mother's passing and only the third encounter with a judge in the entire 15 months of the temporary guardianship. The first judge was not seen again for 15 months after the very first hearing when she allowed my mother to approach the bench, made some small talk, listened to her beg not to be put in guardianship, and then proceeded to put her into temporary guardianship - despite her pleas not to. The errors mentioned in the appeal above were a key part of the initial sections of the complaint in the lawsuit. These errors carried over from the guardianship case, as the same judge who handled the fee-related matters in the guardianship case now presided over the will contest in the probate court.

Following my mother's passing, her estate was transferred from guardianship status to Temporary State Administration while my siblings contested her will. They were feeling very confident in their ability to have me removed as the 1st Executor in my mother's will, given the close relationship with the court-appointed attorneys and their aligned agendas. They were all set to use the same game plan as in the guardianship case—perpetuate the same false allegations and add new lies, but this time, my son, who was the second in line, was in the line of fire too. Their goal was to keep it in the hands of the administrator by converting his "Temporary Administrator" title to "Permanent Administrator," which in their minds would have given them unrestricted access to her estate, especially her house. Shockingly, an attorney was overheard discussing their intention to sell the house and use the funds to cover their legal fees.

Lessons Learned!

1. I loved my parents with all of my heart. I was very proud of their academic accomplishments, and I realized and appreciated the sacrifices that they made for me, the trust and confidence they instilled in me to have a career that is honorable, provides financial security, and most importantly improves the lives of others.

2. My first goal in life is to fulfill God's purpose for me on this earth.
3. The second goal is to please and honor my parents and the family that I now have in addition to my parents.
4. There is no shame or guilt in the way that I have lived my life, the choices that I've made that align with my goals, or with pleasing and honoring my parents.
5. People (including my siblings and niece) made decisions in their life that were far-reaching and negatively impacted their earning potential and ability to participate in mainstream society. Sometimes those decisions are difficult but not impossible to overcome, and sometimes they are catastrophic. I've learned not to judge because "but by the grace of God go thee/me."
6. With empathy and compassion for my siblings' plight, I have to protect my loved ones from being swallowed up in the vortex that comes with addictive behaviors, which leads me to the last lesson learned-
7. "Don't carry baggage that you didn't pack!" (Rev. Howard John Wesley). The issues of my siblings and niece are theirs to own.

Actionable Steps

- Analyze your family dynamics.
- With empathy and compassion, try to figure out the driving force behind those that are disgruntled. Is it fear, financial, jealousy, insecurity, some other negative emotion, or a combination of the above, including a mental health disorder.
- Seek family therapy. If addiction is involved – rehab is a must as well as therapy for the affected family members.
- Parents with young children – pay attention to their dynamics. Sibling rivalry is normal, but if it is prolonged, intense, or crosses the boundaries of what is considered normal – get help ASAP, because whatever negativity is brewing – it gets worse with age and time.
- Parenting is a science, and we know more now than we did a generation ago. Make healthy parenting and family life a top priority, which includes recognizing when a member of your family needs help and getting the assistance that they need right away.

- Take care of yourself, physically, emotionally, and spiritually so that you will have the tools and energy to parent effectively.
- Engage in activities regularly that support an active family life and good health.

We are now in the probate court – different battleground – same judge.

CHAPTER 2. THE PROBATE SYSTEM UNVEILED

Probate is a legal process that takes place after a person passes away to administer their estate. The probate court oversees the probate processes. It involves validating and distributing the deceased person's assets, paying off any outstanding debts, and transferring ownership to rightful beneficiaries or heirs. The probate process ensures that the deceased's final wishes (if they left a will) or state laws (if there is no will) are followed in the distribution of their assets. If there's a will, the probate court appoints the person or institution named by the deceased as executor of the estate. If there's no will, the court appoints an administrator.

Here are the key steps typically involved in the probate process:
1. **Petition:** The process starts with the filing of a petition in the appropriate probate court. This petition requests the court to initiate the probate proceedings and officially

appoint a personal representative or executor to administer the estate.

2. **Notification:** The court provides notice of the initiation of the probate proceedings to interested parties, such as potential beneficiaries, heirs, and creditors. This is typically done through formal notification, allowing them to make a claim, present objections, or assert their rights.

3. **Appointment of Personal Representative if There is a Will, (This Person is an Executor):** The court reviews the petition and any objections raised, and if everything is in order, appoints a personal representative/executor. This person is responsible for managing the probate process, gathering assets, paying debts, and distributing the estate according to the will or state laws.

4. **Asset Inventory:** The personal representative/executor identifies, takes control of, and inventories all the assets of the deceased. This includes real estate, bank accounts, investments, personal possessions, and any other property owned by the deceased.

5. **Valuation of Assets:** A proper valuation of the assets is conducted to determine their worth. This involves

appraisals, assessments, or professional evaluations to establish the accurate value of each asset.

6. **Debt Payment:** The personal representative is responsible for identifying and paying any outstanding debts or obligations of the deceased. They must ensure that all valid debts are fulfilled before distributing the remaining assets to beneficiaries.

7. **Estate Distribution:** If there is a valid will in place, the estate is distributed to the beneficiaries named in the will according to the deceased's wishes. If there is no will (known as intestate), state laws govern the distribution to the deceased person's heirs. The court oversees the process to ensure fair and equitable distribution.

8. **Final Accounting and Closing:** Once the debts have been paid, all assets have been distributed, and all legal requirements have been met, the personal representative/executor prepares a final accounting of the estate's administration. This accounting details all the transactions, payments, and distributions made during the probate process. After the court approves the final accounting, the probate process is concluded, and the

estate is officially closed. It's important to note that the probate process can vary by jurisdiction, as different states or countries may have specific laws and procedures. Additionally, the complexity and duration of the probate process can depend on various factors, including the size of the estate, the presence of a valid will, and the existence of any disputes or complications.

Probate can be a lengthy and costly process. It's public, meaning anyone can see what was owned and owed, who will receive the assets, and what they are worth. Because of this, some people choose to avoid probate through various means, such as owning property jointly, creating living trusts, or designating beneficiaries on insurance policies and retirement accounts.

The Role of the Judge in Estate and Trust Cases

In estate and trust cases, the role of a judge is multifaceted and crucial. Their responsibility is to oversee and manage the legal proceedings related to the distribution of a deceased person's assets and the administration of their estate.

The Probate System Unveiled

Here's a breakdown of the key responsibilities and tasks performed by a probate judge in such cases:

1. **Jurisdiction and Authority:** The probate judge has the authority and jurisdiction (the power to make legal decisions and judgments) to hear and determine matters related to estates and trusts, including wills, testamentary (related to or appointed through a will) documents, and property distribution.

2. **Validating the Will:** The probate judge reviews the will to determine its validity. They ensure that it meets the necessary legal requirements and is executed properly according to state laws. In situations where there is ambiguity or confusion in the wording of a will or trust, it falls to the judge to interpret the document and determine the intent of the deceased or the person who established the trust. If someone dies without a will (intestate), the judge will apply the state's laws of intestacy to determine how the estate should be distributed.

3. **Appointing Personal Representatives or Executors:** The judge appoints a personal representative or executor to manage the estate. This person is responsible for

carrying out the instructions in the will, paying any outstanding debts and taxes, and distributing assets according to the court's orders.

4. **Administering the Estate:** The probate judge supervises the administration of the estate. This involves monitoring the actions of the personal representative, reviewing their accounting and distribution plans, and ensuring all debts and taxes are paid, and that the remaining assets are distributed according to the will's instructions. Dependent executors are required to have more oversight from the judge than independent executors. My mom's will appointed executors who were independent.

5. **Approving Accounts and Distributions:** The executor or trustee is required to provide regular accounting of the estate or trust's assets, debts, distributions, and any other transactions. The judge reviews these accounts to ensure they are accurate and that the executor or trustee is fulfilling their fiduciary duties. Again, this applies more to executors who are dependent.

6. **Resolving Disputes:** A significant part of the judge's role involves resolving disputes that may arise about the estate

or trust. This may include challenges to the validity of the will or trust, claims by creditors, and disagreements among beneficiaries or executor/trustee. The judge listens to arguments from all parties involved, considers evidence and legal arguments, and makes a ruling based on applicable laws. It is also a duty of the court to determine if disputes or contests to the will are brought in "bad faith" (refers to a legal challenge to the validity of a will that is initiated with malicious intent or without any genuine legal grounds).

7. **Interpreting Ambiguous Provisions:** In cases where the will or trust contains ambiguous or unclear provisions, the probate judge interprets the intent of the deceased person and makes decisions accordingly. This helps to prevent disagreements among the beneficiaries and ensures the estate is distributed fairly.

8. **Finalizing the Distribution:** Once the personal representative has completed their duties, the probate judge approves the final distribution of assets to the beneficiaries. This may involve transferring ownership of property, distributing funds, or fulfilling any other

instructions outlined in the will or trust. Again, the applicability of this provision differs between the independent executor and the dependent executor.

Overall, the role of a probate judge in estate and trust cases is to provide a legal framework for the orderly distribution of assets, protect the rights of beneficiaries, and ensure that the wishes of the deceased person are carried out fairly and lawfully.

Common Issues and Controversies Within the Probate System

The probate system handles the distribution of a deceased person's estate, but it is often criticized for various issues and controversies.

Here are some common problems that frequently arise:
1. **Will Contests:** One of the most common controversies is when someone contests the validity of a will. This can occur if beneficiaries feel that the will was forged, the deceased person lacked the mental capacity to make a

valid will, or if there was undue influence, coercion involved in its creation, or fraud. Will contests often result in disputes, requiring the probate judge to evaluate evidence and decide. The credibility of the contestants and their complaints should be taken into consideration.

2. **Disputes Among Beneficiaries:** Conflict between beneficiaries can occur when they disagree on how the estate should be distributed or when there are ambiguities in the will or trust wording. For example, disputes over the interpretation of certain provisions or disagreements related to specific assets can arise, leading to legal battles and the need for the probate judge to intervene and make decisions. As will be discussed later, disputes between beneficiaries should not overrule compliance with the testator's expressed wishes.

3. **Real Estate Issues:** With probate properties, common title issues include errors in public records, outstanding liens or mortgages, and boundary disputes.

4. **Claims By Creditors:** During the probate process, creditors have the opportunity to make claims against the estate for any outstanding debts. Disputes may arise if the

validity or priority of these claims is questioned. The probate judge must assess the legitimacy of creditor claims and determine the amount, if any, that should be paid from the estate.

5. **Appointment of Personal Representatives:** The selection of the personal representative or executor can be a contentious issue, especially if family members or other interested parties have differing opinions on who should assume this role. This can lead to disputes and legal challenges, necessitating the involvement of the probate judge to make the final appointment. In the detailed discussion to follow, in the state of Texas, family disagreements do not give the judge the right to change the executor appointed by the testator except in very special circumstances, including but not exclusively having a felony record.

6. **Delays and Lengthy Proceedings:** The probate process can be time-consuming, sometimes taking months or even years to complete. Probate cases can sometimes become protracted due to various factors, such as complex estates, disputes among parties, or a backlog of cases in the court

system. Delays in the probate process can cause frustration and disputes among beneficiaries or personal representatives/executors, highlighting the need for efficient management by the probate judge.

7. **Lack of Transparency or Issues with the Executor:** Sometimes, the designated executor refuses their role, or there may be problems with how they handle the estate's assets. In extreme cases, assets may be difficult or impossible to find. In some instances, beneficiaries may feel that the personal representative is not disclosing or managing the estate's assets properly. This lack of transparency can lead to suspicions of mismanagement or even fraud. The probate judge may need to investigate and take appropriate actions to ensure the estate's assets are handled appropriately.

   a. This can be a double-edged sword. Family members can express contempt and distrust towards the assigned executor for reasons unrelated to the validity of the will or the decedent's right to choose their trusted executor. These family members may submit frivolous complaints that have no legal basis, wasting the court's time and resources. This behavior also depletes the value of the estate.

    b. The judge has a responsibility to fairly examine both sides, uphold the integrity of the will execution process, and respect the deceased person's rights and wishes. Frivolous complaints should be dismissed promptly, and fraudulent allegations and complaints should be met with sanctions.

8. **Cost:** Probate can be expensive, with court costs, attorney fees, and executor fees potentially consuming a significant portion of the estate's value.

9. **Publicity:** Probate proceedings are public records, which means sensitive information about the deceased's assets and debts, as well as the identities of the heirs, becomes publicly accessible. These issues highlight some of the reasons why many people seek to avoid probate through strategies such as creating living trusts or designating beneficiaries on accounts.

It is important to note that these issues and controversies can vary depending on the jurisdiction, the complexity of the estate, and the specific circumstances of the case. The role of the probate judge is to address these issues, listen to all parties involved, weigh the evidence, apply the relevant laws, and make fair and impartial decisions to resolve the disputes.

Lessons Learned!

The Texas Code of Judicial Conduct states the following:

"Our legal system is based on the principle that an independent, fair, and competent judiciary will interpret and apply the laws that govern us. Judges, individual and collectively, must respect and honor the judicial office as a public trust and strive to enhance and maintain confidence in our legal system."

1. Starting this journey, I had the same faith in the legal profession as most patients have in their doctors. However, I was blindsided by what appeared to be corruption that was pervasive. From my perspective, the judge and appointed attorneys showed no respect for the ethical standards and guidelines governing guardianship, particularly those regarding care and the best interests of

the individual involved. It was an uphill battle when it seemed to me as if they were united in their lawlessness and greed, targeting the only person my mother relied on to fulfill her needs.

2. I learned not to ignore red flags, as they seldom turn green. (Teena Jones)

3. Spotting and confronting "bad faith" situations is crucial. Don't ignore or tolerate them. You may succeed in some cases and fail in others, but overall, it will make people more aware and catch the attention of the judge or jury.

Actionable Steps

- Learn the Rights of a Ward (if you find yourself in a guardianship contest). (See Rights of a Ward in Texas in References.)
- Familiarize yourself with the Estate Codes for your state (full set of codes in References).
- Familiarize yourself with the TX Rules of Civil Procedure (or the similar rules for your state). (See in References.)
- Be familiar with the roles and responsibilities of the appointed attorneys.

- Speak up anytime things aren't going the way you expected or as outlined in any of the references on the guardianship manual. (See References.)
- Recognize and confront acts of "bad faith" without hesitation.
- Exercise your right to file motions or ask for a hearing.
- This process is fast-paced and requires "bulldog" attorneys. During the interviewing process, establish that their strategy and timelines are ones that you are comfortable with. Change attorneys if your team is not aggressive or doesn't seem to be moving the ball.
- Do the best that you can to take care of your loved one's emotional needs and fight like hell to meet other needs (e.g., medical, spiritual, and social).
- Keep a diary or journal of events.
- Have legal consultants available.
- Take care of yourself and prepare for the long run.

CHAPTER 3. THE BATTLE CONTINUES

Account of the Initial Court Proceedings

The court proceedings started with my siblings contesting my mother's will. The will stated that everything should be divided four ways between the four siblings. I was named the 1st Executor, my son was named the 2nd Executor, and my sister's son was named the 3rd Executor.

The common reasons that wills are contested are the following:

1. **Lack of Testamentary Capacity, Also Known as Lack of Mental Capacity:** This is one of the most common reasons for contesting a will. It refers to the mental state of the person when they wrote the will. If it can be proven that they did not fully understand what they were doing, the will may be deemed invalid.
2. **Undue Influence:** If it can be proven that the person was coerced or manipulated into writing their will in a certain

way, it can be contested. This is often difficult to prove but can render a will invalid if successful.

3. **Fraud:** If someone tricks the testator into signing a document they believe is something other than a will, or lies about the contents of a will to get them to sign it, this is considered fraud.

4. **Improper Execution:** Every jurisdiction has specific rules about how a will must be executed. This usually includes being signed in the presence of at least two witnesses. If these rules aren't followed, the will can be contested.

5. **Revocation:** If a more recent will or codicil is discovered, it may challenge the validity of a previous will, leading to a contested probate process. A will can also be contested if it can be proven that the testator revoked it. This could be done by creating a new will or physically destroying the original.

6. **Ambiguity in the Will:** If the language of the will is unclear or ambiguous, it may be contested. If there are errors, inconsistencies, or unclear provisions in the will, it may be contested on grounds of mistake or ambiguity, as

The Battle Continues

the intentions of the testator may not be accurately represented. This often leads to disputes among beneficiaries about the testator's true intentions.

7. **Estrangement and Disinheritance:** Disinherited family members or individuals who were estranged from the testator may contest the will out of a belief that they were unjustly omitted from the distribution of assets.

8. **Claims of Dependency:** In cases where dependents or individuals who were financially reliant on the deceased feel they were not provided for adequately, they may contest the will and claim that proper provision was not made for them.

9. **Delay or Missed Deadlines:** If statutory time limits for contesting a will are not met, a challenge to the will may be dismissed due to procedural issues.

My siblings made the following claims:

1. **The will was forged**—even the Notary. My niece (the one who instigated the false claims and guardianship) and a friend of hers were the two witnesses. She claimed that her signature, her friend's signature, and the Notary stamp and

39

signatures were forged! (At best, this is an argument for "bad faith" at worst – "perjury.")

2. **Undue influence**—my mother's explicit and very vocal trust in me was spun into undue influence.
3. **Lack of testamentary capacity**—eight years earlier, my mom was taken off of the blood thinner that she was on for five days to have a colonoscopy. She had atrial fibrillation (common irregular heartbeats which put people at risk of having a stroke. It is treated with a blood thinner). During those five days, she had a very mild stroke. Strokes are scored by the National Institutes of Health Stroke Scale according to severity, prognosis, and long-term or short-term neurological deficits requiring rehabilitation.

This is how they are scored:
Very Severe: >25
Severe: 15 – 24
Mild to Moderately Severe: 5 – 14
Mild: 1 – 5

Outcomes Related to National Institutes of Health Stroke Scale (NIHSS) Score at Admission[3]

- Scores of <5; 80% of stroke survivors will be discharged to home.
- A score between 6 and 13 typically requires acute inpatient rehabilitation.
- Scores of >14 frequently require long-term skilled care.

Very fortunately, my mother's score was < 5. She was discharged after two days in the hospital, put back on her blood thinner, and did fine for the next eight years.

Another divine intervention was that the lawyer who drew up the will was now a judge and was the only witness who was asked to testify on my behalf. I found out that I only had one witness after the deadline to submit a witness list had expired. That was a significant setback, as I was looking forward to filling the

---

[3] NIHSS stands for National Institutes of Health Stroke Scale. It is a standardized tool used to assess the severity of strokes and the effectiveness of treatment interventions. The score obtained from the NIHSS helps in determining the appropriate management and care for stroke patients.

courtroom with all of my friends and colleagues who would testify to my close relationship with my mother, her unwavering trust in me, knowledge of the money that I happily spent on her behalf, and observations of how I took care of her, especially after my father passed.

My mother and I had been raked through the coals during the guardianship process. My siblings and niece told lie after lie. It seemed to me that they succeeded in their goal to put my mother in temporary guardianship with their alignment with the court-appointed attorneys and aimed to keep her there because they had complete control and I had none. They were blinded by their jealousy of me and disdain for my mother for not thinking more highly of them. She loved them but did not trust them until the end when she told me that the sight of them made her "sick to her stomach." She remained fully aware of the predicament that she was in, which she compared to being in prison and being in Russia. She and I witnessed their sadistic behavior (defined as seeing someone in pain that you have caused and enjoying the experience). It was "evil" personified.

As seen through the lens of my experience, their agenda was perfectly aligned with the court-appointed attorneys, according to conversations that I had with my mother and personal observations, treated my mother like a "nonperson," and deceptively had her labeled as incapacitated and later as having Alzheimer's. They rendered her incapacitated without a single court decision, and in the case of Alzheimer's—there was not a single test or imaging study done, as required to make this clinical decision. It was all made up by my siblings and the attorneys who were determined to keep her in guardianship. The stated goal of the family members, that was documented in court transcripts, was to keep her estate in state administration. This served the attorneys by incurring fees that eventually would drain the value to the lowest number possible. One of the court-appointed attorneys made a statement that the house was going to be sold and attorney fees would be attached.

The family members' goal was to keep it in state administration—out of my hands. They didn't realize that keeping it in state administration was costly and diminished their share as ¼ estate beneficiaries, or maybe they did and didn't care because they were so blinded by hate. My poor niece got nothing except a grandmother who couldn't stand her or her mother when she left this earth. She had no standing in the division of the estate, and she was devoid of lies that could change that fact, as hard as she tried. Was she used by her mother and uncle? You make the call.

My mother told me that she would rather die than stay in the situation that she was in. She did on January 1, 2019, and was finally out of the prison and hellhole that she was living in.

When we got to probate court to fight the will contest, the estate was still in state administration. My siblings accelerated their lies and having a court that leaned in their favor, it was projected that they would win and the estate would remain with the state of Texas. For me, I witnessed my mother's plea for her freedom and her wish that our relationship should not be disrupted fall on deaf ears in the court and with the attorneys who were supposed to protect her. Instead, she was isolated, medically neglected, and persecuted. Now, I was about to witness her Last Will and Testament trampled on. The hard work that my mother and father did all of their life to leave a legacy for themselves and their children was about to go out of the window and up in smoke. They were looked at as two people whose lives didn't matter, except for what could be extracted from their estate. That was unacceptable!!! I decided at that moment to adopt the mantra that I developed and have lived by from this experience:

"Never accept the unacceptable."

And that was unacceptable to me.

Preparing For a Will Contest Trial

Typically, several steps are taken leading up to a will contest trial. While the exact process may vary depending on jurisdiction, the following steps are generally involved:

1. **Determining Standing and Grounds:** The first step is to determine whether you have the standing to contest the will. This usually means that you are either a beneficiary in the will being probated or an heir under state intestate succession laws. Grounds for contesting a will, as previously mentioned, may include lack of testamentary capacity, undue influence, fraud, or improper execution.

2. **Consultation With an Attorney:** The person contesting the will (the contestant) will typically consult with an attorney who specializes in estate litigation. The attorney will review the case and advise on the merits of contesting the will.

3. **Investigation and Gathering Evidence:** The attorney will conduct a thorough investigation into the circumstances surrounding the will, including meeting with potential witnesses, obtaining relevant documents, and gathering any other evidence that may support the contestant's claim.

4. **Filing a Petition or Complaint:** The attorney will prepare and file the necessary legal documents with the appropriate court to initiate the will contest. This may involve filing a petition or complaint, outlining the grounds for contesting the will, and the relief sought. The probate court process is handled at the state and local level, so you should file your claim in the county where the decedent lived at the time of their death.

5. **Service of Process:** After filing the petition or complaint, the court will issue a summon or other notice that must be

served on the named defendants, typically the executor or personal representative of the estate, and any other beneficiaries named in the will. Proper service ensures that all parties involved are aware of the lawsuit and have an opportunity to respond.

6. **Pre-Trial Discovery:** This phase of the proceedings allows each party to obtain information and evidence from the other side. It may involve written requests for documents, interrogatories (written questions) to be answered under oath, and depositions (out-of-court sworn testimony) from witnesses or parties involved. Discovery can help gather additional evidence and build the case.

7. **Pre-Trial Motions:** Before the trial, both parties may file various motions with the court. These motions could include requests to dismiss the case, requests for specific evidence to be excluded, or requests for summary judgment, among others. The court will rule on these motions, which can shape the issues to be decided at trial.

8. **Settlement Negotiations or Alternative Dispute Resolution:** At any point during the pre-trial stage, the parties may engage in settlement negotiations or try

alternative dispute resolution methods such as mediation or arbitration. These processes provide an opportunity for the parties to resolve the dispute without going to trial.

9. **Pre-Trial Conference:** The court may schedule a pre-trial conference to discuss the case with the parties and their attorneys. This conference typically addresses administrative matters, such as establishing deadlines, identifying contested issues, and potentially encouraging settlement. If a settlement is not reached, the case goes to trial.

10. **Trial Readiness:** In the period leading up to the trial, both sides will prepare their case by organizing evidence, identifying witnesses, and finalizing legal arguments. This involves reviewing all relevant documents, consulting with expert witnesses if necessary, and ensuring all necessary witnesses are available and prepared.

These are general steps; the specific procedures and timelines can vary depending on the jurisdiction and local rules. It is crucial for the contestant and their attorney to consult with legal professionals familiar with the specific laws and procedures governing will contests in their jurisdiction.

During the guardianship hearing to contest the fees, the judge, in my opinion, demonstrated a bias and disregard for my complaints and the courtroom antics by the appointed attorneys that were unprofessional and unethical. This led to me filing an appeal. While the appeal was still pending, the will contest trial began.

The challenges that I faced during the pre-trial and the trial which informed my decision to sue the judge and later to go *pro se* were as follows:

1. I requested a jury trial because the conduct of the judge that led me to file an appeal undermined my confidence in getting a fair bench trial. The judge polled my siblings who were on a roll from the guardianship proceedings. They all voted for a bench trial because according to my sister, she was tired of the process and wanted to go and see her "grandbabies." Despite my request, the judge went with the majority, and I was denied a jury trial. This was problematic because as per the Sixth Amendment to the

United States Constitution, individuals have a constitutional right to a trial by jury in criminal cases and in civil cases where the amount in controversy exceeds $20. This right can be waived if both parties agree to a bench trial or if the court determines that a jury trial is not necessary based on the nature of the case. When it comes to will contests, which are typically civil cases, the decision of whether to have a jury trial is generally dependent on the rules and procedures of the specific jurisdiction. There are no rules or procedures that dictate that a majority rule can deny a party's right to a jury trial. Besides, much more than $20 was at stake. The judge defied my constitutional right for a trial by jury in favor of the opposing parties who were in the majority.

2. The second challenge was that my attorney elected to not call any witnesses that could testify to my character and my relationship with my mother. Specifically, to testify that our relationship was genuine and not subject to undue influence. I was prepared to fill the courtroom with witnesses. That was a setback that strengthened the

opposing side. Also, a neurologist expert witness was not called, nor were any of the many physicians who had taken care of my mother for years, who could testify that her stroke was mild and that there were no cognitive or physical sequelae. There also would have been credible testimony from the network of doctors that she saw regularly that she was not incapacitated and certainly didn't have Alzheimer's.

3. During discovery, my attorneys, at great cost to me, found the Notary that notarized the will. My niece's signature was in the record book that he kept of all notarizations. That was proof that my niece's signature was not forged and the notary was not forged.

4. The attorney who drew up the will is now a judge. He still had the original will on his office hard drive which matched perfectly with the will that was presented to the court—proof that the will was not forged.

Justice Served: How I Represented Myself to Victory

Notes from the Bench Trial

During a grueling and unjustifiable cross-examination that lasted a day and a half, I faced continuous, baseless attacks on my credibility. False accusations and defamatory insinuations were thrown at me relentlessly, without any fact-checking. To add to the difficulty, I found myself in the challenging position of serving as both an expert witness for my mother's medical condition and as her daughter, all while being a pediatrician specializing in critically ill newborns. Despite this conflict, I relied on my extensive knowledge of strokes in newborns, which was acquired through my comprehensive medical training and extensive experience. I tapped into my understanding that the mechanism of strokes in newborns is similar to that in adults, as well as my background in reviewing the medical records of adults who have experienced strokes for insurance companies. With these resources, I successfully defended myself amidst the intense questioning and demonstrated my competence in this complex field.

The evidence presented for undue influence centered around the birthday party that I gave on her 88th birthday. My niece claimed she wasn't invited to the party, implying that I deliberately excluded her. However, the truth was that I didn't know how to contact her, so I asked her mother to inform her about the celebration. Unfortunately, she failed to do so and concealed from her daughter the real reason behind the lack of invitation.

Another instance of alleged undue influence was when my mother asked my niece to move out after initially agreeing to let her stay for six months. The request came as a result of my niece failing to maintain cleanliness and letting the room become unsanitary with spoiled food. My mother had graciously provided her with a place to live due to her homelessness, under the condition that she move out in six months. During the court proceedings, my niece claimed that I forcibly evicted her from the house, using it as evidence of my undue influence. However, the truth was that my mother decided to establish boundaries and hold my niece accountable for her actions and commitment to move in six months, and we were at the over one-year mark. I was present when my mother made this decision, and it had nothing to do with any coercion or manipulation on my part. The accusation of undue influence was merely an attempt to shift blame onto me for my mother's protective actions.

Similar to the guardianship proceedings, I sensed that my voice was overshadowed and disregarded. The relentless stream of lies and false insinuations went unchallenged, leaving no opportunity for a counter-defense. My only witness was the current judge who wrote my mother's will. He testified to her capacity of drawing up a will and understanding of the contents in it. When my siblings and niece were cross-examined, they lied about checks that they had forged from my mother's account. The perjury that they committed on multiple occasions went unchecked.

The Verdict and My Decision to Sue the Judge

The judge walks into the courtroom to give his verdict and mumbles you're not going to like this. He was right!!! His verdict was that the will was valid and would be probated accordingly, but I was disqualified as the 1st Executor because of the family rancor. He then took another poll about whether the estate should stay under the Administration of the State. Again, it was unanimous that the estate should go to the State of Texas for administration.

My sister's son was the third in line as executor. In solidarity with the evil majority, he stepped down from his executor position and testified that he was in favor of the estate going to the State of Texas for administration. Everyone was elated and thought that this was now a done deal! They had got what they wanted through their lies – I was removed as executor. That was the only reason for the contest because the will stated that everything would be equally split four ways. Right before the high-fives, a bombshell was dropped. My son was the 2nd Executor. The judge was caught off guard when he was told this. His response was

"Is that Sheila's son?"

A resounding "YES" echoed through the courtroom. The judge then responded that he (my son) would have his day in court, but he believed that no one would qualify as the executor in the family. A hearing was set 45 days later to determine the fate of my family estate. I was advised that he would disqualify my son and assign a dependent executor to administer the estate. In Texas, there are two types of executors:

An independent executor and a dependent executor. They are primarily distinguished by the degree of court supervision they require during the probate process, particularly in states like Texas.

Here's a breakdown:

1. **Independent Executor:** An independent executor is able to administer an estate with minimal court supervision. They can sell assets, pay debts and taxes, and distribute the remaining estate to beneficiaries without having to seek court approval for every action. This can accelerate the probate process and reduce costs. However, an independent executor still has a fiduciary duty to manage the estate responsibly and in the best interests of the beneficiaries.

2. **Dependent Executor (Non-Independent Executor):** A dependent executor, on the other hand, must get court approval for many actions during the probate process, such as selling estate assets or paying the estate's debts. This

type of executorship is typically used in more complex estates or when there's a potential for disputes among heirs or mismanagement of the estate.

The executors in my mother's will were independent. The court-appointed dependent executor would charge the estate a fee for their services, which in our case was up to $350 per hour. The independent executors would not charge a fee, another major difference.

After the guardianship hearing and the bench trial with this judge, it became clear that I was going to lose the estate and my mother's last wishes were going to be ignored. I pondered,

"Did I really win?"

My legal team regarded this as a win since the will was admitted. My answer, however, was NO. My mother would not get her first or second choice of executors for her will. That was unacceptable to me and was the last straw. I had already lost my mother; I wasn't going to lose her estate or let them deny my late mother her constitutional right to have her wishes honored in her Last

Will and Testament. The legal option offered to me was to let the verdict play out and then go to the court of appeals. This could take years, during which time the house would be sold and there would be nothing left of the estate to claim. Even if the house was not sold, it would have been taken over by either Harris County for delinquent property taxes or the IRS for back taxes. Neither of these scenarios were acceptable.

In fact, I decided that I was going to do anything necessary to reverse the tide and get the estate back into the family with one of the executors she named. I decided to sue the judge and file a motion for his recusal before the next hearing date in 45 days.

Lessons Learned!

1. The probate court's flaws are systemic and pervasive throughout the process, from guardianship to will admission and execution.
2. My mother's case demonstrated that elder's rights, due process, and constitutional rights are being blatantly disregarded, while the deceit, lies, and betrayal of family

members seeking financial gain continue to go unchecked. This destructive trend gets stronger with each victory.

3. In my case, and in the case of many others that I have spoken to in this situation, a powerful alliance is formed between the disgruntled family members and the ethically compromised attorneys. This bond creates a formidable barrier against justice. When this happens, the courts are manipulated to harm the vulnerable victim and anyone attempting to defend them.

4. The checks and balances are inadequate and easily overridden.

5. In my opinion, this is a legalized form of "trafficking the estates of the elderly." Although not a widely recognized or standardized legal term in this context, it seems appropriate to associate this term with the fraudulent or unethical practices related to the management of an elderly person's estate, that results in the transfer of wealth from a family's estate to the coffers of court-appointed attorneys and the state directly and indirectly to judges - who, in Harris County are elected officials and benefit from campaign contributions made by the attorneys that

they appoint. These offenses also meet certain criteria for RICO when they are committed at an "enterprise" level. Applying this term and concept to the elderly and their estates may be complex, but it is still relevant.[4]

6. Don't wait too late to figure out that you are in over your head. Make adjustments – a) change your legal team, b) put everything on pause to get adequate legal counsel, or c) go *pro se* (represent yourself)[5].

---

[4] The Racketeer Influenced and Corrupt Organizations Act (RICO) is a U.S. federal law that provides extended criminal penalties and a civil cause of action for acts performed as part of an ongoing criminal organization.

While RICO is often associated with cases involving organized crime, it can also be applied to any instance where individuals or organizations engage in patterns of illegal activity as part of an "enterprise." This could potentially include cases of elder financial abuse if it involves systematic fraudulent or criminal behavior.

For example, if an individual or organization is systematically exploiting seniors, perhaps through scams, fraud, or undue influence to gain control of their estates, and they do this as part of a wider criminal enterprise, then they might be prosecutable under RICO. The key here is the existence of a pattern of racketeering activity that is part of an "enterprise."

[5] "*Pro se*" is a Latin phrase that translates to "for oneself" or "on one's own behalf." In a legal context, it refers to individuals who represent themselves in court without the assistance of a lawyer.

This could happen in any type of legal proceeding, including civil lawsuits, criminal cases, divorce proceedings, etc. While courts often advise against *pro se* representation due to the complexities of the law and legal procedures, they also recognize the right of individuals to represent themselves.

Actionable Steps

- Assess your legal team.
- Discuss their strategy and all potential outcomes, and make sure that you are 'OK' with their assessment and plan.
- If you're going to trial, make sure that you have witnesses, including experts to testify on your behalf.
- Make sure that your attorneys are prepared. Anticipate the opposition's strategy and have a rebuttal plan.
- Have a plan to fact-check in real time. Don't hope that the judge or jury will deduce when a party is lying.
- Ensure that your lawyers call out perjury immediately and highlight credibility issues with the opposing team and arguments presented. For example, it was never revealed that my sister was a current and life-long heroin addict

---

It's important to note that *pro se* litigants are held to the same standards as attorneys in terms of court rules and legal procedures. This means they need to understand and follow court rules, file the appropriate legal documents, present evidence, and make legal arguments just like a trained attorney would.

While some people choose to represent themselves to avoid legal fees, it can be risky because of the potential for unfavorable outcomes due to a lack of legal knowledge or experience.

which drove her lifestyle, her attitude toward our parents and me, and her chronic desperation for cash. The same for my youngest brother.
- Listen to your gut. Are you on the defense or offense? You want to be on the offense!
- Check for a clause in the will for contesting in bad faith. If this is the case and your lawyer doesn't fight for it – insist on it or change lawyers.
- Make sure that each of the tasks required for prepping for trial are done thoroughly.
- Develop a checklist that will serve as your project management tool.

This is most of all that you will need.

CHAPTER 4. PREPARING TO WAGE WAR

My first step was to try and find an attorney who specialized in judicial misconduct and was willing to take my case. I called law firms all over Texas and not a single one would take my case. The reasons given were the political fallout that would ensue, and they were unwilling to take on judges, who have very broad immunity. Everyone thought that the chance of winning was 0%. I then made the decision to go *pro se*. I owed it to my parents and their legacy to fight. The second step was to conduct legal research on how to go *pro se*, how to sue a judge, and finally how to file a motion for recusal.

I first had to learn everything there was to know about going *pro se*, starting with the definition. *Pro se* is a Latin phrase that means "for oneself" or "on behalf of themselves." In legal terms, it means a person represents themselves in court without an attorney. *Pro se* litigants are held to the same standard as attorneys, which seems very daunting at first but becomes easier with experience, practice, and time.

The pros of going *pro se* include:
1. Saving money.
2. Getting your day in court.
3. The court will hear your voice and your story.

Some cons of representing yourself in court include:
1. There's no buffer between you and the court.
2. You may not be able to evaluate or anticipate legal issues.
3. You may not be able to negotiate a plea deal.
4. The court, including the staff, can be patient at one extreme and hostile at the other end to people who decide to represent themselves and go *pro se*.

In my case, saving money was a big plus, as I had almost exhausted my savings account, and I didn't think that I would have enough money to stay in the race which promised to be a long one. Unfortunately, many victims find themselves in this situation and are forced to give up earlier than they would have otherwise because of the financial drain.

Having my voice heard was an unexpected advantage. I was never comfortable putting my case totally in someone else's hands—regardless of their reputation. They don't know my story like I do, and they'll have to squeeze my story and case into a plethora of cases they already have. Inevitably, something gets lost in translation. During the whole guardianship process, I had to sit back and let other people talk for me, and as good or bad as they may have been, I always think that I am my best advocate and I represent myself the best. Having my day in court was more liberating than the feeling that I was totally out of my league and could potentially be chewed up alive and spit out by real lawyers. My voice had never been heard before – literally. Now was my chance, and I relished the opportunity.

The cons of going *pro se* didn't matter because I had no choice. After weighing the options, this was the only way. I also discovered that if a lawyer has reservations about your case and the path that you want to take, they do you a favor by not taking it on, and you save a lot of precious time and money. Sometimes, it is not apparent that you and your lawyer are on different pages; a conflict that can't be resolved.

This experience has taught me to ask questions that are very relevant to my case and to my expectations for possible outcomes. I will share more in my final thoughts.

Now, I'm on the bona fide *pro se* path to my goal of getting out from this judge's court. The next step is doing legal research on how to reach my goal.

Overview of the Legal Research Conducted

When you google "Can I sue a judge?", you will find variations of the following response: **Generally, NO.** There is a doctrine called judicial immunity that prevents most lawsuits against judges when they are acting in their judicial capacity. Judges have absolute immunity for actions they take in their judicial capacity. This means that judges are not individually liable for the judicial acts they perform, including the decisions that they make in court.

https://publiccounsel.org/wp-content/uploads/2021/11/Guide-Can-I-Sue-a-Judge.pdf/

If a judge made a decision that you disagree with, filing an appeal may be the proper course of action and is an alternative to filing a lawsuit. There are very strict time limits for filing an appeal. In Texas, the time limit to file an appeal can vary depending on the specific circumstances of the case. As a general rule, the deadline to file a notice of appeal is 30 days after the judgment was signed (Texas Rules of Appellate Procedure - TRAP 26.1). However, in some cases, the deadline can be as short as 20 days after entry of the judgment. It's important to note that if you miss these deadlines, you may lose your chance.

A different type of appeal, known as a restricted appeal, must also be filed within 30 days after the date of the final judgment. A restricted appeal, also known as a bill of review, is a type of appeal in Texas that can be pursued when no timely post-judgment motions are filed and no notice of appeal is filed within the 30-day deadline after the judgment was signed. This type of appeal allows a party to challenge a judgment after the normal

deadlines have passed, under certain specific conditions. To prevail on a restricted appeal, a party must show that:
- They filed their notice of restricted appeal within six months after the judgment was signed.
- They were a party to the underlying lawsuit.
- They did not participate in the hearing that resulted in the judgment in question and did not timely file any post-judgment motions or requests for findings of fact and conclusions of law.
- The error in the complaint is apparent from the face of the record.

A restricted appeal is a complex legal procedure, and it's recommended that anyone considering one should consult with an attorney. It's important to note that a restricted appeal is not a second chance to try a case; it's a way to correct a clear error when the usual appeal procedures were not followed. By following the strict deadlines of the appeal process you should be able to avoid being in this situation. If you are in this situation, you may want to get legal advice because of the legal and logistic complexity.

The final type of appeal is the writ petition, which has different time limits than usual appeals. A writ petition is a formal written request made to a court, asking for a specific judicial action. It's often used as an extraordinary remedy when the usual legal procedures are inadequate or unavailable. The exact time limits for filing writ petitions can vary depending on the type of writ, procedural rules, and jurisdiction.

- **Common Law Writ Petition:** The time limit for filing a common law writ petition is typically governed by the doctrine of laches, usually interpreted as 60 days from the date of the ruling.

- **Writ of Certiorari:** This is a type of writ seeking higher court review of a lower court's decision. The petitioner must file the writ within 90 days from the date of the entry of the final judgment in the United States Court of Appeals. If appealing to the Supreme Court, the petitioner has a certain amount of time to write a brief, not exceeding 50 pages.

- **Writ of Mandamus:** This is a command issued by a court ordering a government agency, court, or official to perform a duty they are obligated to complete. There is no specific time limit for filing a writ of mandamus. However, a petition could be dismissed if the petitioner unreasonably delays in filing it.

- **Habeas Corpus:** This is a writ requiring a person under arrest to be brought before a judge or into court. The Antiterrorism and Effective Death Penalty Act imposes a one-year statute of limitations on habeas petitions.

The last two of the writ appeals are mentioned only for the sake of completing the list. For the habeas corpus, I have only seen and heard of it in crime TV shows. You should not have to file any of these. If you do, I would not recommend going *pro se*. Get a lawyer, a good one!

Finally, in Texas, if you believe a judge in a probate court (or any other court) has engaged in judicial misconduct, you can file a complaint with the **State Commission on Judicial Conduct**. The Commission is the state agency responsible for investigating allegations of judicial misconduct or disability.

Preparing to Wage War

The specific rules for filing a complaint are as follows:

- **Written Complaint:** The complaint must be in writing.
- **Details About the Judge:** The complaint should include the name of the judge and details about the alleged misconduct.
- **Separate Forms:** If you're filing complaints about more than one judge, you should use a separate form for each judge.
- **Evidence:** While not explicitly stated in the rules, it's generally advisable to provide as much evidence as possible to support your allegations.

The Texas State Commission on Judicial Conduct does not specify a statute of limitations for filing a complaint. However, the Commission encourages individuals to file complaints as soon as possible after the alleged misconduct occurs. Once the Commission receives a complaint, it reviews the allegations. If the Commission finds sufficient evidence of misconduct, it may conduct an investigation. Depending on the seriousness of the misconduct, the Commission can take disciplinary actions ranging from issuing a private or public reprimand to recommending the removal or retirement of the judge.

It's important to note that the Commission does not have the authority to change a judge's ruling or decision. Its role is to investigate allegations of judicial misconduct or disability, not to act as an appellate court. As always, you should consult with a legal professional for accurate and up-to-date information and advice tailored to your specific situation.

Up to this point, I have three options:
1. File a lawsuit.
2. Appeal the judge's decision, which is the traditional process and procedure for registering a complaint against the judge.
3. File a complaint with the Judicial Commission.

I already had a complaint against this judge in the appellate court. I could not meet the 45-day time limitation going this route. The probability that this could take years would defeat my purpose because the estate would be liquidated by then. Despite the advice from several attorneys to appeal the judge's decision after he put the estate in state administration, I nixed that option. Also, if I wanted to halt the sale of the house while I was going through an appeal, I would have to put up several hundred thousand dollars in bond. I didn't want to do that either. To be candid, as a non-lawyer, it was very difficult to go against the advice of well-meaning attorneys. Staying focused on my single goal, having a very small supportive network, and time made it easier.

Filing a judicial complaint is always an option, and for some may be the best and only option, depending on your goals. If you want to raise awareness of a problem, this is the best, most comprehensive way to do it. The limitation to this is that the decisions are not reviewed or reversed. It is clearly stated that the commission does not serve as an appellate body. My final decision was to file a lawsuit and a complaint with the judicial commission. I would recommend doing both. As it turns out, the 45-day window that I had to work with gave me only enough time to file the lawsuit and the motion for recusal. When the judge recused himself, filing the complaint with the commission became less important. To cover all bases, I would recommend doing both, because they serve different but complementary purposes.

Legal Research on "How to Sue a Judge?"

"Judges are typically immune from a lawsuit."

You cannot sue judges for actions they took in their official capacity. For example, a judge who decides a case against you cannot be sued.

"Only in rare circumstances can you sue a judge."

This preamble will be the first sentence in almost any online inquiry about suing a judge. I felt that there are exceptions, and my case was one, so I was proceeding forward with it.

You may sue for non-judicial acts. Non-judicial acts are acts which are not normally performed by a judge. Some acts which have been found as "non-judicial" include:

- Making repeated racially charged comments about a party with the hopes of getting people, including the party's attorney, to distance themselves from the party.
- Making repeated derogatory comments to the media about a party.
- Trying to get a party fired from his or her job.
- Physically assaulting one of the parties in the courtroom.

Next, file a complaint also known as a lawsuit. Following the rules of civil procedure, you will have to draft a complaint and file it with the appropriate court. The complaint should allege the facts surrounding the dispute, the legal justification for the lawsuit, and your requested relief. One of the bases of a lawsuit against a judge will probably be the deprivation of civil rights. These suits are called "Section 1983" cases, which is the section of a federal statute that authorizes such hearings.

Section 1983 provides an individual the right to sue state government employees and others acting "under color of state law" for civil rights violations. Section 1983 does not provide civil rights; it is a means to enforce civil rights that already exist.

This was a claim among many others that I included in my lawsuit. The next step will be to defend against a motion to dismiss. The judge will undoubtedly try to get the case dismissed by filing a motion to dismiss. The motion will argue that the judge is protected by judicial immunity, which is absolute. You will need to argue that the alleged conduct was not judicial in nature and that the lawsuit should proceed.

Fortunately, I didn't get to this phase until three months after the recusal—reconfirming that the path that I chose was the only viable option given the limitation of 45 days. I will outline the whole process in Chapter 7 – The Aftermath. The next legal research was on disqualifying a judge.

How to Disqualify a Judge for Bias

Courts have explained that bias is a favorable or unfavorable opinion that is inappropriate because it is not deserved, rests upon the knowledge that the judge should not possess, or because it is excessive. The remarks made by the trial judge must reveal a high degree of favoritism or opposition making it impossible for the defendant to have a fair outcome.

In the Supreme Court case **Liteky V. United States**, (See: https://www.supremecourt.gov/pdfs/transcripts/1993/92-6921_11-03-1993.pdf German-American citizens were on trial in an espionage case. During the proceedings, the judge presiding over the case commented that German-Americans have hearts "reeking with disloyalty." This comment was found to be biased and reflective of a trial judge displaying partiality.

Bias, though, does not encompass unfavorable rulings, expressions of impatience, dissatisfaction, annoyance, or anger. During the trial, if the judge makes critical, disapproving, or hostile comments to the counsel, parties, or about their cases, this still does not support a claim of bias.

The Constitution is applicable to all citizens of the United States, whether the defendant or the judge. If a judge displays bias in any trial, as defined in the above information, he/she is not immune from having their actions examined. (https://www.robertguest.com/what-is-judicial-bias.html#)

The Importance of Understanding Legal Jargon and Court Procedures

Understanding legal jargon and court procedures is crucial for individuals representing themselves in court proceedings, also known as *pro se* litigants. Without a legal background, navigating the complex legal system can be challenging. Familiarity with legal terms and court procedures is necessary to effectively advocate for one's rights and present a persuasive case. Legal jargon, also known as legalese, often encompasses complex terminology and language that can be difficult for laypeople to comprehend. However, comprehending this language is essential since it can affect the outcome of your case. Misunderstanding a term or phrase can lead to errors in filing paperwork, presenting arguments, or understanding what is happening during proceedings.

Court procedures, on the other hand, dictate how legal cases progress through the court system. They encompass everything from how to file a lawsuit to how to present evidence and argument in court. Understanding these procedures is important

Preparing to Wage War

to ensure fairness and impartiality. A lack of familiarity with court procedures can result in delays, case dismissals, or unfavorable rulings.

Here are some examples of legal jargon and important court procedures that *pro se* litigants should be aware of:

1. **Legal Jargon:**
    a. **Burden of Proof:** The obligation to provide sufficient evidence to support a claim or defense.
    b. **Motion:** A written or oral request made to the court during the proceedings, usually seeking a specific action or decision.
    c. **Discovery:** The process of obtaining evidence from the opposing party before trial, through methods such as interrogatories, requests for documents, and depositions.
    d. **Hearsay:** Out-of-court statements offered as evidence to prove the truth of the matter asserted, generally inadmissible unless falling under an exception.
    e. **Precedent:** Previously decided cases that serve as a basis for interpreting and deciding similar cases.

2. **Court Procedures:**
   a. **Pleadings:** The initial documents filed by parties in a lawsuit, including complaints, answers, counterclaims, or motions.
   b. **Service of Process:** The official delivery of legal documents to the opposing party for providing notice of the lawsuit.
   c. **Pretrial Conference:** A meeting between the parties and the court before trial to discuss case management, settlement possibilities, and procedural matters.
   d. **Opening Statement:** A statement made at the beginning of the trial, outlining the facts and issues involved in the case.
   e. **Cross-examination:** The questioning of a witness by the opposing party after they have been questioned by the initial party.

Pro se litigants should also be aware of local court rules, deadlines for filing documents, rules of evidence, and proper courtroom etiquette. Failing to understand these aspects can lead to procedural errors or disadvantages in presenting your case. By understanding legal jargon and court procedures, *pro se* litigants can effectively communicate their arguments, address the court appropriately, and present their case in a way that is understandable and persuasive. Additionally, proper understanding enables them to better respond to the opposing party's arguments and objections, enhancing their chances of success in the courtroom.

The American Bar Association asserts that the rules of procedure apply to all parties, including *pro se* litigants. Therefore, it's essential for *pro se* litigants to educate themselves on these procedures to ensure they are following them correctly. In conclusion, understanding legal jargon and court procedures is vital for *pro se* litigants. It not only helps them navigate the complex legal system but also ensures they get a fair opportunity to present their case.

Lessons Learned!

1. Managing a seemingly daunting and overwhelming process with little margin for error is possible.

2. Life and death situations in my profession of critical care medicine demand a methodical approach. The same holds true in the legal arena, where mindset and preparation play a key role in being successful.

3. I discovered how going *pro se* paid off with multiple rewards, including the acquisition of essential skills that can positively impact the lives of others - a mission dear to my heart and my parents' legacy.

4. Saving money on legal fees enabled me to go further and delve deeper into the probate system, uncovering intricate relationships and issues. The increased knowledge facilitated greater exposure.

5. Deciphering the complex language and excessive wording found in legal writing becomes less daunting with time and increased experience.

6. It is important to master the legal lingo, procedures, and protocols that rule the court's everyday operations. Equally important is a thorough grasp of deadlines and the ability to comply with them.

7. Unlocking your limitless potential is as simple as having a clear purpose, a vividly imagined goal for the future that

you are trying to create, and a tight-knit support system. Together, these invaluable assets will propel you through the times that are challenging and isolating.

Actionable Steps

- o Learn the jargon.
- o Learn the procedures and the processes.
- o Set up important dates in a special calendar.
- o Consider setting up a separate email, so that important emails are not missed or overlooked.
- o Decide to go *pro se* or not. Again, this is a marathon, not a sprint. The decision to go *pro se* can happen at any time or not at all, depending on your circumstances.
- o Choose the best channel to register your grievance(s)/complaint(s). This may include, the State Commission on Judicial Conduct, filing a lawsuit, or filing an appeal on a decision that was legally or ethically flawed (not just the one that you disagreed with or didn't like. The judge has immunity to cover those decisions).

Justice Served: How I Represented Myself to Victory

(**Note:** When following any of the legal procedures presented in this section, please consult an attorney or certified legal advisor to evaluate the credibility, suitability, and legality of such steps.)

CHAPTER 5. FILING THE LAWSUIT

The Step-by-Step Guide that I Followed:

Step 1:

My first step was to put a support team together. During my research of organizations with the mission of stopping probate abuse and elder abuse, I was referred to a journalist who wrote stories on this topic and had in fact been involved in challenging an unconstitutional guardianship of a family member. She had also gone *pro se* during part of her journey. She made filing the lawsuit against the judge easier for me by sharing the knowledge that she gained from her experience, as well as from the experiences of others that she wrote about. She shared some of the actual filings that she had done *pro se* and was very instrumental in giving me the courage to go forward. She also chronicled my journey in a series of articles - starting the first article with my filing of the lawsuit. This was helpful in raising awareness.

The second person is my first cousin, Donald Owens. He was my closest friend as I went through the very painful guardianship and the eventual death of my mother. He patiently listened to the blow-by-blow details and remained a solid source of support when I had anxiety attacks about suing a judge. I would call him very early in the morning or in the middle of the day just so he could say "You are doing the right thing." Once I called him at 3 pm in the middle of the week, and I asked the rhetorical question for the hundredth time,

"Am I doing the right thing?"

His reply was,

"It is criminal if you don't file this suit and at least try to get your family's estate back."

I never asked that question again or felt the need to. I was moving forward with the wind at my back propelling me with a force, momentum, and resolve that I knew would not let me turn back - nor did I want to.

His sister, Regina Owens, was equally as supportive and quickly became the sister that I always missed having.

Step 2:

The next step was to find a lawyer who would provide consultation services. I learned that there are organizations that provide these services. I have listed a few of them in the References. I chose to engage a freelance lawyer from one of those services, and after interviewing several, I settled on one who was an excellent choice for this vital part of the work. I knew my story well and could do the best job of putting it in writing. His job was to connect the story to my legal claims and provide case studies that substantiated my claims. I gathered the evidence, kept track of the deadlines, and made sure that the writing of the lawsuit was in the proper format.

A decision had to be made regarding the claims to be added to the case and the best court to file it – state or federal? Since discrimination was a part of the claim, a Section 1983 lawsuit was filed in federal court.

Step 3:

The next step was gathering evidence. I used the following sources to gather evidence:

A. Motions that were filed by my attorneys, which included contesting the fees of the court-appointed attorneys and the demand for a jury trial that was denied.

B. The briefs that were filed in the appellate court. These documents were crucial because they outlined all of the errors that the judge (aka the court) made during his tenure of presiding over the guardianship hearing. The errors were based on expert witness testimony and court documents. The expert witness testified how each appointed attorney individually and collectively failed to fulfill their duties in a guardianship that my mother was thrust into without a hearing or any due process to which she was entitled. Specifically, I believed that the TG isolated my mother and violated her American with Disabilities protection by taking away a phone that I bought her that paired with her cochlear implant (my mother was functionally deaf) so that she could have conversations with friends and family and see them on FaceTime. That action furthered her isolation. The TG also banned visits from her close friends, family, and sources of support – pending background checks which never happened; thus, the ban was never lifted.

The TG also allowed her health insurance and long-term care insurance to lapse, medically neglected her, and colluded with her daughter (my sister) and granddaughter (my niece) to keep my mother in guardianship. She repeatedly misrepresented me to the other appointed attorneys and single-handedly weaponized the court against me. She caused my mother to be labeled as being incapacitated by sending a physician to do an Independent Medical Exam (IME)[6] on her while she was hospitalized.

---

[6] An Independent Medical Examination (IME) is a medical assessment performed by a healthcare professional, usually a doctor, who has not previously been involved in the person's care. The purpose of an IME is to provide an impartial opinion about the individual's health status.

When it comes to determining competence, an IME can be particularly useful if used appropriately. Competence, in this context, refers to an individual's mental capacity to understand the nature and effects of one's acts. This could include the ability to make informed decisions about one's own healthcare, financial management, or legal matters.

There was no hearing for the IME as required, and the physician was rude to my mother and to me when I called him to ask why he was examining her. He replied that he was asked to do an IME (by the TG) and that she "flunked" like he thought she would. The TG later told a different story and said that she sent the physician to see my mother in response to the several requests that I made that she be allowed to follow up with her geriatric psychiatrists who had diagnosed her with PTSD after being put in the guardianship. She was caught making a statement that was shockingly false. The TG was planning on putting my mother in permanent guardianship and she sent an unethical, unprofessional physician to do her bidding. She later presented my mother as a "diagnosed" Alzheimer's patient without any medical exam or imaging studies to substantiate that diagnosis.

The hospice medical director confirmed that Alzheimer's was written all through her chart.

Lastly, while an IME can provide valuable information, it's just one piece of the puzzle. Other factors, like the individual's behavior over time and the opinions of those close to them, should also be considered when determining competence.

The expert testified that the attorney ad litem did absolutely nothing to keep my mother out of guardianship or get her out once she was placed there. She testified in court that when she interviewed my mother "she was talking good" and didn't seem to have any problems. She was also standing by her in the courtroom as my mother was pleading not to be put in guardianship or disrupt her relationship with me. She was perfectly lucid but said nothing to defend her as the judge placed her into temporary guardianship. Even after the court investigator recommended that my mother did not need or want to be in guardianship, the AAL did nothing to further her cause, despite evidence to the contrary. She did not file a single brief, motion, or anything to support my mother. Her inaction then and throughout the year signaled her agreement with the actions of the TG to make sure that I did not get guardianship and that my mother would not get out of this hell hole.

The GAL called me when he was first assigned and told me that he "heard" that I caused a raucous at my mother's cardiology appointment. Before I could respond, he said it doesn't matter, you are not going to get the guardianship. The week before, I made an appointment to take my mother to her cardiologist because she was having increasing shortness of breath. The TG insisted that my niece come to the appointment with me. Through my attorney, I objected because I knew that this would upset my mother, yet it was to no avail. She was aware that her daughter and granddaughter were responsible for her being in this situation and didn't want any contact with them. During the appointment with the cardiologist, my niece barged into the examination room. My mother got very upset and asked her to leave. She refused because the TG told her to come. That made my mother more furious. Eventually, I calmed my mother down and my niece gave her the privacy that she asked for.

The TG told her fellow appointed attorneys that I caused the raucous according to her discussion with the doctor. I

Filing the Lawsuit

had taped the whole episode and distributed it to all of the attorneys. It was then that she walked back her statement and said that the niece/granddaughter was confused. This was direct evidence of how she was lying to malign my character in the view of the court and the appointed attorneys. The GAL, acting on the misinformation that he received from the TG, later called my attorney delusional and instructed her to withdraw my application for guardianship. He also said that he was not going to look at the financial records that exonerated me from the false claims that were made against me of financially exploiting my mother. That was his duty that he abdicated. In the end, all three attorneys filed a joint objection to my financial records based on a statute that was not applicable to my case.

On this backdrop, the appellate brief pointed out five points of error:

    i.   The trial court abused its discretion in awarding almost $20,000 to the guardian ad litem who had not properly performed the duties of that role and whose fees were not reasonable and necessary.

ii. The trial court abused its discretion in awarding over $53,000 to the temporary guardian who had not properly performed the duties of that role and whose fees were not reasonable and necessary.

iii. The trial court erred in approving the second amended final account of the temporary guardian which was not signed.

iv. The trial court erred in awarding fees for services to the TG for her own interest. She hired an attorney to represent her in the fee contest hearing. The court allowed the money for payment to be taken out of my mother's estate, which is definitely against the guardianship statutes. This was a personal, non-guardianship-related expense.

v. The trial court abused its discretion in awarding $15,000 to the attorney ad litem, who had not properly performed the duties of that role and whose fees were not reasonable and necessary.

The trial court overruled all of the challenges and awarded appointees approximately $90,000 in fees and expenses. The court signed off on some of the orders and fee deductions from the estate without proper notice to me. The guardianship was abruptly closed without a notice to me. A "finding of facts and conclusions of law" was requested twice and ignored.[7] The abrupt ending of the guardianship without notice, the perceived arrogance of ignoring our requests for a "finding of facts," and the recklessness of signing off on $90,000 with total disregard for their failure to perform their duty was too much to ignore. This was furthered by a proclamation from the GAL that he

---

[7] "Finding of Facts, Conclusions of Law" is a legal term used in the court system. Here's what each component means:

Finding of Facts: This refers to the process where a judge reviews evidence and testimony presented during a trial or hearing and determines the facts of the case. It's essentially the judge's interpretation of what happened based on the presented evidence. The judge's findings of fact are usually detailed in a written decision or judgment.

Conclusions of Law: Once the facts are determined, the judge applies the relevant laws to those facts to reach 'conclusions of law.' This involves interpreting the law and deciding how it applies to the specific facts of the case. It also includes determining which party is legally at fault or liable.

In other words, "finding of facts, conclusions of law" is the process by which a judge decides a case: first by determining the facts, and then by applying the relevant laws to those facts.

didn't have a responsibility to perform the duties of a GAL. One of the motions was not signed by or served on me. He didn't care and signed off anyway. I also alleged that the judge lost the courtroom decorum by allowing the GAL to spew inflammatory, defaming, and unsubstantiated allegations at me in his defense of his abdication of his responsibility to my mother and the court.

C. **Court transcripts were important pieces evidence.** I was able to back up the events of the guardianship hearing, as well as the events during the will contest with the court transcripts. In addition to disqualifying me as my mother's 1st Executor, the court transcript captured the judge's remark about my son having his day in court, but he didn't think that any family member was qualified to serve as executor because of family rancor.

D. **Evidence of the lapse in health** and long-term care insurance was presented.

E. Disqualifying my mother's designated first and second independent executors was evidence in my defense that my mother's constitutional rights were violated - once again. The rulings of several Texas Supreme Court cases were presented.[8]

---

[8] One notable Texas Supreme Court case that emphasized the importance of complying with a testator's wishes is "Matter of Estate of Russell," which was decided in 2007. In this case, the court reaffirmed the principle of "testamentary freedom," meaning that a testator has the right to dispose of their property as they see fit through a valid will. In the "Matter of Estate of Russell," the court held that a testator's clearly expressed intentions should be given effect, even if they conflict with traditional rules of law or public policy, as long as they do not violate any legal constraints. The court emphasized the significance of honoring a testator's right to determine the distribution of their assets after death. It is worth noting that there have been other Texas Supreme Court cases that support the importance of respecting a testator's wishes.

Here are a few more Texas Supreme Court cases that have supported the importance of honoring a testator's wishes:

1. "Estate of Lee": In this case, decided in 1997, the court emphasized the testator's freedom to dispose of their property as they desired, as long as the will complied with statutory requirements. The court upheld the testator's right to make specific bequests and distribute assets according to their wishes.
2. "Reininger v. Schriner": In this 2009 case, the court reiterated the principle that a testator's intent as expressed in the will should be respected, as long as the will was executed properly and followed legal requirements. The court emphasized that courts should be cautious about interfering with a testator's intended disposition or rewriting the terms of a valid will.
3. "Bates v. Strehli": This case, decided in 2016, emphasized the importance of giving effect to the testator's plain and unambiguous language in the will. The court held that if the language of the will is clear and unambiguous, the court should not interpret or alter the terms but rather enforce them.

These cases, along with others, highlight the significance of the testator's intentions and the court's role in upholding their wishes as expressed in a validly executed will.

Justice Served: How I Represented Myself to Victory

In summary, I described the judge as being reckless in approving monies to be paid out of my mother's estate with total disregard for the evidence that they did not perform their duties, including signing off on invoices that were unsigned and paying for the personal representation of an attorney that was not involved with the estate. A guiding rule is that a court may not award fees to be paid from the ward's estate for an appointee to represent their own interest. An appointee defending their fee request is representing their own interest, not that of their client. Also, there are case law rulings by the Texas Supreme Court that discuss fees charged to the ward's estate.

This was followed by a refusal to state the rationale behind his decisions (Finding of Facts and Conclusions of Law) after two requests. I made the argument that this behavior betrays public trust in the integrity of the legal system.

Facing these sets of facts, and the clock ticking toward the total loss of everything my parents spent their lives working for with the intention of leaving it to their four children, not strangers in the Harris County Probate System; I took a deep breath, said a prayer for strength, received validation from a very few selected people inside my circle, and ignored the large circle of naysayers who predicted that bad things would happen to me. To make sure that I knew as many facts as I needed to know, I asked,

"What is the worst thing that can happen?"

I was told that I could be sanctioned. My research revealed that the sanction amount would be $1,000.00. I also determined that this is not a crime punishable by capital punishment (most important) or even jail time. My cousin Donnie told me that it would be "criminal" for me not to file a lawsuit and defend my parent's legacy—so I "just did it"!

Template for Filing a Lawsuit in Federal Court

Filing a lawsuit in federal court requires specific documents and forms to be filed. Here is a basic template to help you get started:

[Your Name] [Your Address] [City, State, ZIP Code] [Phone Number] [Email Address] [Date]

Clerk of Court [United States District Court] [District Name] [Address] [City, State, ZIP Code]

Re: [Case Name and Number]

Dear Clerk of the Court, I, [Your Name], the plaintiff in the above-captioned case, am hereby filing a lawsuit in the [United States District Court] located in

1. **Civil Cover Sheet:** This form provides basic information about the case and the parties involved. It can be obtained from the court's website or the clerk's office.
2. **Complaint:** Attached is a copy of the complaint, detailing the allegations and legal claims against the defendant(s). The complaint sets forth the specific facts and legal grounds for the lawsuit.
3. **Summons:** Enclosed is a completed set of summonses for each defendant. The summons must be properly served on each defendant, notifying them of the lawsuit and providing them with a specific time frame to respond.
4. **Filing Fee:** I have enclosed the required filing fee as per the court's instructions. If a fee waiver or installment plan

is available, please provide the necessary forms for consideration.

5. **Notice of Appearance:** If applicable, I have included a notice of appearance for any attorney representing me in this matter.

6. **Exhibit List and Exhibits:** If any exhibits will be introduced as evidence in the case, please find an enclosed exhibit list and the corresponding exhibits.

I kindly request that you file and docket these documents accordingly. Please provide confirmation of the case information and any additional instructions for further steps in this process.

Thank you for your assistance. If you require any additional information or forms, please do not hesitate to contact me.

Sincerely,

[Your Name]

Please note that this template serves as a starting point, and it is important to review and comply with the specific rules and requirements of the federal court where you are filing the lawsuit. It may be beneficial to consult an attorney for guidance in preparing and filing the necessary documents.

(**Note:** When following any of the legal procedures presented in this section, please consult an attorney or certified legal advisor to evaluate the credibility, suitability, and legality of such steps.)

Template for Completing the Complaint Section

When preparing a federal lawsuit, it's important to include the following information and sections in your complaint:

1. **Caption:** The caption states the name of the court, the case number, and the names of the parties involved (plaintiff and defendant).
2. **Jurisdictional Statement:** This section explains why the lawsuit falls under the court's jurisdiction. It may include references to federal laws or the Constitution that grant the court authority to hear the case.
3. **Parties:** This section describes the plaintiff(s) and defendant(s) in the case, providing their full legal names,

addresses, and contact information. It's essential to accurately identify all parties involved in the lawsuit.

4. **Facts:** This section outlines the relevant facts of the case in a clear and chronological manner. Include detailed information about what happened, when it occurred, and any parties' actions or omissions that are relevant to the claims being made.

5. **Legal Claims:** This section sets forth the specific legal claims or causes of action against the defendant(s). Each claim should be clearly stated and supported by applicable legal theories or statutes.

6. **Requested Relief:** Clearly state what you are seeking from the court as a resolution or remedy. This may include monetary damages, injunctive relief, or any other specific actions you are requesting the court to take.

7. **Exhibits:** If applicable, reference any supporting documents that are relevant to your case. Attach these documents as exhibits, such as contracts, photographs, or official records, and refer to them within the complaint as evidence supporting your claims.

8. **Signature:** At the end of the complaint, leave a space for your signature and date.

It's important to note that this is a general outline, and the specific format and requirements for federal lawsuits may vary depending on the court and jurisdiction. It is crucial to consult the Federal Rules of Civil Procedure and any local rules specific to the court you are filing in to ensure compliance. Additionally, consulting with an attorney experienced in federal litigation can be highly beneficial in drafting and preparing a lawsuit to ensure its validity and effectiveness.

(**Note:** When following any of the legal procedures presented in this section, please consult an attorney or certified legal advisor to evaluate the credibility, suitability, and legality of such steps.)

Initial Reactions and Responses

The naysayers were silent, with the exception of one who called me and railed for two minutes on how whoever wrote the suit for me to sue a judge should be disbarred! He missed the irony of the lawsuit being filed by me, and I can't be disbarred as a non-lawyer! The best way to describe my inner circle was that we were steadfast and committed to stay the course because this was only the first step to reclaiming my family estate. I had to get the case out from under this judge. The only way was to make a case for his recusal – voluntarily or by court order after a hearing. Of course, the former was preferable, but I was prepared for the latter too.

The judge responded with his obligatory "Response to the Complaint." He denied all of the allegations, in spite of the detailed evidence that was submitted to support each count. Summarily, he claimed the expected excuse of having "judicial immunity" that protects him from all decisions made in the capacity of being a judge.

The conclusion of the first step of filing the lawsuit led to the second important and strategic step of filing a motion for recusal – my next chapter—figuratively and literally!!

Lessons Learned!

1. The significance of assembling a support team cannot be understated. Team size is not the determining factor; what truly matters is their ability to provide both support and information.
2. Evidence plays a crucial role in leveling up your case. With meticulous documentation - notes, emails, court transcripts, filed motions, and appellate court briefs—you can flawlessly piece together a powerful complaint supported by solid case laws.
3. The template provided reassurance that I was following the correct guidelines and regulations, while also efficiently organizing the required information.

Actionable Steps

- Reassess your support team – to include:
    - Friend(s)
    - Family
    - +/- Therapist
    - Freelance Lawyer Consultant

- Avoid naysayers. Their negativity can be very distracting and debilitating.
- Gather all the facts that will be used for evidence.
- Plug the information into the template for filing a complaint.
- Be prepared to answer responses (on time).
- File for a recusal.
- Be prepared for either possible outcome – a voluntary recusal or a hearing before an administrative judge.

(**Note:** When following any of the legal procedures presented in this section, please consult an attorney or certified legal advisor to evaluate the credibility, suitability, and legality of such steps.)

CHAPTER 6. MOTION FOR RECUSAL

Explanation of What a Motion for Recusal Is

A motion to recuse a judge is a legal procedure that seeks the disqualification or removal of a judge from a case. It is typically filed by one of the parties involved in the litigation, alleging that the judge has a conflict of interest, bias, or some other reason that would prevent them from impartially presiding over the case. Here are the key points to understand about a motion to recuse:

1. **Grounds for Recusal:** There are various grounds upon which a party can seek recusal. Common grounds may include:

    a) **Personal Bias or Prejudice:** If a judge has a personal relationship with one of the parties, their attorney, or a witness that may cause bias or an appearance of bias.

    b) **Financial Interest:** If a judge has a direct or indirect financial interest in the outcome of the case.

    c) **Previous Involvement:** If the judge has previously been involved in the case as an attorney, witness, or in any other capacity that could affect their impartiality.

d) **Public Statements or Conduct:** If a judge has made public statements or engaged in behavior that raises doubts about their ability to fairly adjudicate the case.

e) **Other Circumstances:** Any other circumstances that could reasonably affect the judge's ability to be impartial, including situations where the judge's independence or integrity may be compromised.

2. **Filing the Motion:** The motion to recuse is typically filed with the court where the case is being heard. It should clearly state the grounds for recusal, providing specific facts and evidence to support the belief that the judge should be disqualified.

3. **Judicial Review:** Once the motion is filed, the judge in question will review the motion and may have the opportunity to respond. They will evaluate whether the grounds presented are valid and whether they should recuse themselves from the case.

4. Decision on Recusal: The judge will make a ruling on the motion to recuse. If the judge agrees and voluntarily recuses himself/herself, another judge will be assigned to the case. If the judge denies the motion, the case will proceed with the judge in question continuing to preside over the proceedings. It's important to note that the standards and procedures for filing a motion to recuse can vary depending on the jurisdiction and court rules. Consulting with an attorney who specializes in litigation can help guide you through the process and determine the best course of action based on the specific circumstances of your case.

The procedure to file a motion for recusal of a judge in the Harris County Texas probate court can be found within the Texas Rules of Civil Procedure, specifically Rule 18a. Here are the steps:

1. A party may file a motion with the clerk of the court stating the grounds for the recusal or disqualification of the judge. The motion must mention the basis for the claim for which the judge should be recused.

2. This motion must be filed as early as possible before the beginning of the trial or other hearing if a judge is believed to be biased or prejudiced. Specifically, before the 10th day of the next trial or hearing.
3. The respondent judge then has the option to voluntarily recuse themselves or refer the matter to the regional presiding judge.
4. If the judge voluntarily recuses themselves or if a motion for recusal or disqualification is granted by an administrative judge, the case will be referred to a judge in another court to preside over the case.
5. If a party files a motion alleging that another party in the case filed a motion for the recusal or disqualification of a judge solely to delay the proceedings, the court may impose sanctions against the offending party.

Please note that this process is subject to change and it is always recommended to consult with a legal professional or the court's clerk's office directly for the most accurate information. "Recusal and Disqualification of Judges, Tex.R.Civ.P.18a" is provided in its entirety in the Resource section.

Sources

- Recusal and Removal in Statutory Probate Court
- Tex. Gov't Code § 25.00255
- Rules of Probate Court
- Recusal and Disqualification of Judges, Tex. R. Civ. P. 18a

(**Note:** When following any of the legal procedures presented in this section, please consult an attorney or certified legal advisor to evaluate the credibility, suitability, and legality of such steps.)

Case Timeline

I operated on the following timeline:

- Trial dates – 9/11/2020 - 9/14/2020
- Decision by the Judge – 9/21/2020. The will was admitted to the court as being a valid will, however, the 1st named Executor is disqualified because of family rancor. The 2nd named Executor was mentioned, and when he learned that he was my son, declared that he had concerns about him

getting it also. The 3rd Executor was the son of the disgruntled sibling, and one of the instigators of the will contest. He declined to be an executor and expressed his vote for the estate to be turned over to a permanent administrator. The disgruntled family members were polled and it was unanimous that the estate should be turned over to the State.

- Hearing Date (to *officially* turn the estate over to the State for permanent administration) – 11/9/2020.
- Lawsuit filed – 10/21/2020.
- Motion for Recusal filed – 10/28/2020.
- Deadline for the judge to respond – 11/2/2020 (3 business days from receipt of the motion, 7 days before the next scheduled hearing).
- **Response from the judge to voluntarily recuse himself was received at 4:59 pm on 11/2/2020!**

This Is How I Made My Case

1. **Facts Were Presented from the Lawsuit Filed One Week Earlier**

a. Approval of excessive claims for expenses and reimbursement from my mother's estate at the hearing to contest the fees. My mother was an elderly citizen with the disability of total deafness who was owed and denied protections under the Americans with Disabilities Act. She had an iPhone that paired with her cochlear implant that was taken away from her by her temporary guardian, who refused to give it back despite pleas from me and my attorneys explaining how this act isolated her. This demonstrated a bias toward the court-appointed attorneys.

b. Lack of transparency in giving an explanation of why he ruled the way he did despite two requests.

c. Statements received from disgruntled family members were made in open court at the hearing to contest the fees by the guardian ad litem, which were untrue, inflammatory, defamatory, and uncivil. The judge did little to bring civility, truth, and honor back into the proceeding, in a way that was not discriminatory.

d. He showed a perceptible bias toward the disgruntled family members by signaling that he was not going to appoint any member of the family – even though there were only two left who were named in the will – me and my son. It should be noted that the others were not named and that my son was a graduate of Yale University and was completing a Psychiatry residency as a Chief Resident at Standford University.

e. He decided that my son was probably not going to be assigned as the 2nd Executor based on the disgruntled family poll, and what felt like his bias against me and my son, because he was my flesh and blood. This opinion was expressed before any evidence to the contrary could be presented at the hearing scheduled for November 9, 2020.

f. Although it was not mentioned, I requested a jury trial for the will contest. I was outvoted by the disgruntled and depraved family members and denied a jury trial. This was a blatant violation of my constitutional right.

g. There were two "coup de gras" that occurred after I filed the lawsuit. The ruling in the fee contest was sent to the court of appeals for review and was still in review at the time that my lawsuit was filed as well as the motion for recusal. My sister's daughter, (the primary instigator of the whole guardianship along with my sister, her mother) sent a letter to the appellate court bragging about how I had been disqualified from being an executor and that my son was probably going to be disqualified also because the judge made the statement that no one in the family would qualify. This was the fifth letter that she had written to the appellate court in support of the court-appointed attorneys and the judge while adding slanderous, defaming, and patently false statements about me. The appellate court finally told her to stop writing them. That was the gift "*of demonstrating the circle of bias from the judge to the* *appointed attorneys and to the family members causing the rancor – and back to the judge."*

h. The second "coup de gras" gift was a random Facebook post from someone that I did not know and had never met. An article was written about my lawsuit and the judge's signaling that my son would not be named as the 2nd Executor based on disqualification because of family rancor, as was the case for his mother. A person made a very short, simple response after reading the article: "B.S. The grandson is a Yale graduate and not fit to be an Executive (sic)?" This was the gift, that *"a reasonable person would think that a judge is not capable of being impartial."*

2. In Addition to the Tex. R. Civ. P., I Presented Two Case Laws to Support My Position:

- *Boyles v. Gresham,* 158 Tex. 158, 309 S. W. 2d 50, 53 (1958).

    The case of Boyles v. Gresham was a Texas probate case that dealt with the validity of a will. The case involved a writing alleged to be a will and was under review for probate. U.C. Boyles, the appellant, offered the document for probate as the holographic will of Lon Gresham, who had passed away. However, its probate was contested by Arch V. Gresham, who claimed to be the son of Lon Gresham.

In the proceedings, it was decided that it was not the court's role to construe the will further than deciding whether it was valid or not. The judge abused his discretion in disqualifying me to be the 1st Executor as per my mother's will. His role was only to admit the will as being valid or not valid, not to change the executors.

- *re Estate of Gober,* 350 S.W. 3d 597, 599 (Tex. App. — Texarkana 2011, no pet).
  Courts have given great weight to the executor chosen by a decedent. There is authority that mere family

conflict and mistrust are not enough.[9] These facts did not justify non-compliance with the Testator's will.

The opinion even has a section entitled "Allegations of Personality Conflict Were Inconsequential." I made the argument that bias and partiality are glaringly apparent as well as total disrespect and disregard for the rights of citizens to name executors and expect that the named executors will be given rights after their death to execute their wishes.

I concluded that the judge's conduct was contemptuous to me. Impartiality is not expected given the past pattern of behavior. "Qualification" under the Estates Code is purely a function of compliance with section 305.002.

Section 305.002 of the Texas Estates Code pertains to the required contents of a will. According to this section, a valid

---

[9] 350 S.W.3d 597, 599 (Tex. App. — Texarkana 2011, no pet). In *re Estate of Gober*, the appellate court held the decedent's daughter was not disqualified even though the evidence showed that she and her brother "don't agree on anything," "don't trust each other at all," and "will never agree."

will in Texas must be in writing, signed by the testator (the person making the will) or by someone else at their direction in their presence, and attested by at least two credible witnesses who are over the age of 14. Furthermore, the testator's signature must be made with the intent of executing the will.

The section of the Texas Estates Code that discusses the qualifications to serve as an executor is Section 304.003. This section outlines the general requirements that an individual must meet to be eligible to serve as an executor of an estate. These qualifications include:

    i.   **Age:** The executor must be at least 18 years old.

    ii.   **Capacity:** The executor must be of sound mind and not be disqualified by a court due to a felony conviction or other legal restrictions.

    iii.   **Residency:** The executor must be a resident of Texas unless they are related to the decedent or the estate's principal place of administration in Texas.

    iv.   **Felonious Conduct:** The executor must not have been convicted of a felony or a crime of moral turpitude unless the court finds it appropriate to waive this requirement.

The named executor is not required to establish any particular skill set or legal acumen as it was suggested at my son's trial. Being named and not "disqualified" under section 304.003 is sufficient. Neither I nor my son met the criteria for disqualification.

3. I Submitted the Following Exhibits to Support My Position

   a. The transcript from the trial was presented demonstrating his reason to disqualify me and the plan to disqualify my son.

   b. The letter by one of the instigators of my mother's guardianship to the appellate court bragging on the judge's action – which was meant to be in total support of the court-appointed attorneys. This closed the circle of collaboration and corruption to my mother's detriment.

c. An article published by a local Houston newspaper about my lawsuit entitled "Doctor Sues Judge Over Guardianized Mother's Will" was published and it outlined my complaints.

d. A second article was presented, again by a local paper that highlighted the corruption in the Harris County probate court: https://www.straighttalkmoney.com/articles/families-go-to-battle-in-probate-court-only-to-leave-without-anything.

e. The Facebook post in response to the article about my lawsuit against the judge which demonstrated that a reasonable person would think that the judge is not capable of being impartial.

4. The Legal Standard for Recusal Was Presented

A summary of the statutes that outline the reasons and the process to ask for recusal and how my case was appropriate. The legal standard for motions to recuse is set out in Rule 18b of the Texas Rules of Civil Procedure, and particularly Rule 18b (1) & (2), which provide in part that "a judge must recuse in any proceeding in which:

(1) the judge's impartiality might reasonably be questioned;

(2) the judge has a personal bias or prejudice concerning the subject matter or a party."

The American Bar Association's (ABA) objective standard: "A judge shall avoid impropriety and the appearance of impropriety."

The ABA Model Code's test for appearance of impropriety is, "Whether the conduct would create in reasonable minds a perception that the judge's ability to carry out judicial responsibilities with integrity, impartiality, and competence is impaired."

The rule does not require that the judge must have engaged in any biased or prejudicial conduct. It does require the judge to recuse if, "his impartiality might reasonably be questioned," regardless of the source or circumstances giving rise to the question of impartiality, even if the source and circumstances may be beyond the judge's volition or control. The judge had no control over the letters to the appellate Court, however, it demonstrated that the granddaughter perceived a special relationship with the judge and the appointed attorneys that was inappropriate.

The Texas intermediate courts of appeals have applied the same objective standard:

The standard for recusal is clear. When the party moving for recusal relies on bias to claim the trial judge should be recused, the party filing the motion to recuse must show that a reasonable person, with knowledge of the circumstances, would harbor doubts as to the impartiality of the trial judge, and that the bias is of such a nature and extent that allowing the judge to serve would deny the movant's[10] right to receive due process of law.

---

[10] In a court of law, a movant is the party who makes a motion. A motion is a formal request presented to a judge for a decision on a particular matter related to the case. The party who initiates this request, either the plaintiff or defendant, is referred to as the movant.

The test for recusal under the Rule [18b(b)] is, "whether a reasonable member of the public at large, knowing all the facts in the public domain concerning the judge's conduct, would have a reasonable doubt that the judge is actually impartial." (The FB response addressed this issue.)

The U.S. Supreme Court cases "tell us that ordinarily actual bias is not required, the appearance of bias is sufficient to disqualify a judge."

As stated above, Texas law requires that a "judge shall recuse in any proceeding in which ... [his] impartiality might be reasonably questioned."

In determining whether a judge's impartiality might be reasonably questioned to require recusal, the proper inquiry is whether a reasonable member of the public at large, knowing all the facts in the public domain

---

The other party is typically called the respondent. The movant seeks a ruling or order from the court, which could be about anything from a request for a change in trial date to a request for a judgment without a trial (summary judgment).

concerning the judge and the case, would have a reasonable doubt that the judge is actually impartial.

In furtherance of the goal of avoiding the appearance of impropriety, the Code of Judicial Conduct provides that the judge "should act at all times in a manner that promotes public confidence in the integrity and impartiality of the judiciary" and "shall not allow any relationship to influence judicial conduct or judgment."

Nor should judges "lend the prestige of judicial office to advance the private interests of the judge or others; or permit others to convey the impression that they are in a special position to influence the judge." (The judge's penchant for polling the disgruntled family members to make his decisions as well as the granddaughter's repeated letters to the appellate court gave the impression of a special relationship with the judge that was inappropriate.)

These concerns stem from the recognized need for an unimpeachable judicial system in which the public has unwavering confidence.

5. The Conclusion and Prayer (Remedy)

The following requests were made pursuant to this motion:

a. That the court (i.e., the judge) voluntarily recuse itself from any further participation in this case;

b. That in the alternative, should the court not voluntarily recuse itself in response to the motion to recuse, that the motion to recuse be referred to a different judge to rule on the referred motion or for assignment of a judge to consider this motion;

c. That in the event a judge is assigned to consider this motion, the assigned judge schedule and conduct a hearing on this motion;

d. That following any such hearing, this motion be granted and the judge be ordered recused from any further participation in this matter; and I also request any other and further relief to which it may show me to be entitled, including, not exclusively;

e. Reconsideration of my "suitability" since a motion has not been entered yet.

Dated: October 2020.

And Signed

Eventually, the judge voluntarily recused himself, which only happens in 9% of all requests. Stated another way, in 91% of the cases, the judges stay on. In some states, there is no recourse. The judge makes a decision on whether he will stay on the case, and if he decides not to recuse himself, he just continues as the presiding judge. In Texas, however, if the judge decides to not recuse himself, I had the right to have a hearing with an administrative judge who would make the final decision. Of course, I was prepared to do that. In this case, the judge and his cabal of court-appointed attorneys and my disgruntled family members made an airtight case that I was able to document in a convincing way. The Facebook post was an unexpected blessing and icing on the cake.

CHAPTER 7. THE AFTERMATH

The judge's recusal required that my mother's case be assigned to another court and a new judge. This had to be done by the County Administrative Judge. There was a palpable rippling effect within the walls of the probate court system. On my side, everyone was stunned and in disbelief! I had accomplished what I could not achieve with the various attorneys that I had hired to represent me because they were unwilling to go down that path, as were the many lawyers that I approached. I understood that I was just one client and they would have to face the judge many times in the future with other clients too. I did not plan to have any other interactions with this judge or court and therefore had nothing to lose except my mother's estate. In the short term, that was enough. There was another hearing to prepare for to determine the executor of the estate. This time, the executor was going to be one of the named choices in my mother's will. The State of Texas was not one of them!

Although it was awkward, I went back to my attorneys to represent me in the hearing and what I thought would be a quick closure to what had seemed to be a nightmare that would never end. I did not have the experience or confidence to speak in court before a judge and represent myself in open court that I now have – and will share with you as we travel down this journey.

There were hours that led into days of meetings with speculations on which way the new judge would rule. Would he just take up where the old judge left off or comply with my mother's will? The majority opinion was that he would just take up where the old judge left off. That didn't sit very well with me, but I was tired and worn down. The fight in me was temporarily waning. I insisted that they at least try to have me reinstated. There was no official hearing where legal arguments could be presented. To do that, they would have to request a hearing where legal arguments could be presented on my behalf. That process was not completed. Their position was that the best use of their time and resources was to fight to have my son appointed as the independent executor.

The Aftermath

We were reassigned to a different court – and a different judge. During the hearing, my son was being considered for the role of independent executor. However, the son of the disgruntled sister also appeared. The judge acknowledged his presence and inquired whether he had declined his position as the third in line for executorship, indicating that he did not wish to be appointed.

In a continuation of the family conflict, he promptly responded, "Yes, but I believe the estate should be entrusted to a third-party administrator." The judge replied, "That would be a no," and swiftly dismissed his suggestion, making it clear that his opinion on appointing a third-party executor was irrelevant. This was quite different from the tone of the previous court proceedings.

The hearing began with an introduction of my son and his illustrious academic career, which included Yale undergraduate and starter on the football team where he was named to the All-Ivy League, Master's in Epidemiology at Columbia University, Medical School at St. Louis University, and Chief Resident in Psychiatry at Stanford University.

He testified that he was financially independent after financial support from me up until he got his first salary as a resident. He said that he was aware of the conflict between his mother and her siblings, but he was sheltered from being in direct contact or in the crossfire. He also stated that he would be fair and execute his grandmother's wishes to the best of his ability and according to her stated desires in the will. Then came the cross-examination, which was brutal and relentless with lies and innuendos. His ability to handle finances was questioned, to which he replied that he would hire an accountant or accounting firm to manage the finances, in the same manner that he has retained an attorney to oversee the legal aspects.

The disgruntled sister's daughter was the star witness – even though she had no standing. There were repeated questions about her not receiving an invitation to the 88th birthday party that I threw for my mother. The truth was that I did not know how to get in touch with her and told her mother to give her the message about the party, which she apparently did not. Her mother let her believe that she was not invited and didn't inform her that she failed to give her the message. My son had nothing to do with the invitation list. She also caused him to be hammered by the fact that he had never lived full-time with his grandmother – as she had because she was homeless.

My son spent as much time as his schedule would allow with his grandparents – which included summer jobs in Houston, medical school electives at Baylor, and taking his required medical school exams in Houston. In addition, as a family, we spent all of our holidays with my parents, went on vacations together, and they attended my medical conferences with me and my sons. My niece, who is 15 years older than my son, started but did not finish college, and she was far from being financially independent. Her jealousy was palpable.

In the end, the judge dismissed the temporary administrator and appointed my son as the independent executor. Finally, my mother's wishes were complied with. Even though I was her first choice, I am sure that she is pleased that her grandson was able to prevail through the courageous efforts of his mother.

For the first time since the start of this journey, I had tears of joy replacing the tears of pain and grief. I knew that this was a Divine Intervention, and I am eternally grateful to God and my parents who I know were looking down on us from Heaven and serving as our Angels of protection and justice.

Lessons Learned!

1. Trust your instincts. As Teena Jones said, "Red flags never turn green." Despite my heroic act of recusing the judge, my attorneys continued to doubt. They believed that the new judge would simply continue where the old judge left off. They questioned appointing my son as the 2nd Executor due to the distrust surrounding him, simply because he is my son. They were unwilling to convincingly present me for reconsideration. They clung to the old way of doing business, which was staying on the defense and on the ready to defend all of the baseless claims that were alleged. They used the siblings' and court's distrust of me to maintain the status quo. I became very disheartened.

2. I "accepted the unacceptable," which was against my motto of effectively advocating for myself.
3. Against the odds, my son's appointment proved that good does triumph, no matter how long it takes. This journey tested my courage like never before, reaffirming my belief in both God and myself.
4. Through this experience, I learned that courts are inept and struggle to identify plaintiffs with mental illness and with perverted ulterior motives, leaving families and the justice system helpless in defending against their destructive influence of paranoia, delusions, and toxic manipulations. Mental illness was always the 800 lb. elephant in the room. There are some lawyers and judges who are either purposely inattentive or corroborating in leveraging their illness and proclivity for constant drama and discord for financial gain. Doing the math, fighting family members are a higher ticket item than those that are not fighting.

Actionable Steps

- Seek professional help from a mental health specialist if you have family members who resemble the ones that I have described in my family.
- Advocate for mental health awareness and early and consistent intervention - at every turn and every level.
- Ask the court to mandate an evaluation and treatment for mental health disorders as part of the remedy that you ask for in your complaints.
- Not intervening is enabling and only serves to worsen the problem by making the complainant feel empowered to continue their dysfunctional behavior - which in extreme cases can cause a person to die prematurely—as was the case with my mother.
- Realize that people with mental illness have little or no insight and are not able to take responsibility for the outcome of their actions which hurt them and other people – especially those closest to them—their families and friends.
- To parents with young children, pay attention to sibling rivalry. Although a normal part of growing up, if it becomes too protracted or intense, seek help immediately. This will not go away and will only worsen with age.

CHAPTER 8. REGAINING THE ESTATE AND TRUST

"Snatching victory from the jaws of defeat!"

Anonymous

Step-By-Step Account of How the Estate and Trust Were Regained

1. Evidence was gathered regarding the judge's non-compliance with the Estate Codes of Texas or the code of conduct expected and mandated by regulatory bodies that provide oversight and that his conduct was adversely affecting me and my case:
   a. Court transcripts.
   b. Copies of motions.
   c. Copies of appellate briefs and responses.
   d. Information on the scope and regulatory authority of the following agencies:
      - American Bar Association.
      - Texas Rules for Civil Procedures.

- Texas Government Code – section 25.00255.
- Rules of Probate Court.
- Code of Judicial Conduct.
  - **The State Commission on Judicial Conduct:** This is an independent Texas state agency responsible for investigating allegations of judicial misconduct. The Commission's jurisdiction does not extend to federal judges and magistrates, administrative hearing officers for state agencies, or the State Office of Administrative Hearings. https://www.scjc.texas.gov/
  - **The Office of Court Administration (OCA):** This body provides staffing and support to judicial branch regulatory boards and policy-making bodies. It also oversees children's courts and the regional presiding judges. https://www.txcourts.gov/oca/
  - **Council of Judges:** In certain counties like El Paso, the Council of Judges is established by the

Texas Government Code for the purpose of overseeing the administration of justice.

County of El Paso Texas - Council of Judges (epcounty.com)

- **County Commissioners Court:** In each of Texas' 254 counties, the county commissioners court serves as the governing body. This administrative body was established by the Texas Constitution.

  https://www.galvestoncountytx.gov/our-county/county-judge/court-functions/

- **The Texas Supreme Court:** The State Bar of Texas is an administrative agency of the judicial department that aids the Texas Supreme Court in the regulation of the practice of law.

  https://www.texasattorneygeneral.gov/opinions/categories/1131/

Please note that these bodies generally oversee state and local judges. Federal judges are overseen at the national level by bodies such as the Judicial Conference.

You will have to find the regulatory bodies, procedural rules, and probate court rules for your state.

Furthermore, a lawyer was engaged for consultation. (A list of organizations and companies that offer free or low-cost legal services is available in the Resources.)

2. Research cases from the appellate courts (state, district, and regional), state courts, and US. Supreme Court. A lawyer can help with the research as well as crafting the legal documents that will be required to be filed.

3. Craft your story in your own words, adding your personal interpretations of the events. If consistency is not your strong suit, consider keeping a diary or journal to stay organized. Additionally, make use of your email

correspondence as a reliable timeline of events. Once your narrative is complete, it's time to enlist the help of a freelance lawyer who can transform it into a legally sound document using the appropriate language and writing style. This task may not come naturally to non-lawyers, but fear not, as the lawyer will also assist in finding relevant case laws to support your position.

Working as a team, you will handle the necessary writing tasks – writing the complaint, rebuttals to the responses that will follow, and appeals. These were the steps in the lawsuit which continued for the next six months. The motion for recusal had to be filed at the same time the lawsuit was in process. Freelance assistance is helpful for that important task. So, when the first judge recused himself, and we were in a different court, the lawsuit was still going on. I did not have to speak in court until we had a scheduling conference for a trial. I only needed to speak a few sentences, primarily agreeing to the timetable set by the judge leading up to a trial, if there was one. Much later,

I have had to write motions and defend them at a hearing. I am getting more comfortable with each experience. I am always aware and very thankful for the money that I am saving, as well as the confidence that I have gained with speaking my truth and being on the offense for the first time.

4. Following the assignment of a new judge and different court, a hearing was held to determine the independent executor of my mother's will.

5. The opposing family members aggregated around the lies that were told during the will contest and manufactured new ones. Their strategy to disqualify him was the following:
   a. He was not an accountant or lawyer.
   b. He had never lived with his grandmother full-time, despite the fact that he was always working or in school.
   c. His Yale tuition was somehow stolen from my mother's account. An allegation made by his uncle who

has struggled all of his life with alcoholism, chronic unemployment, and stints in jail for smuggling drugs across state lines.

d. His cousin (the granddaughter instigator) was my mother's favorite.

e. He excluded her from a birthday party that he did not sponsor, nor did he have any control over the invitation list.

His lawyer did not call any witnesses on his behalf, which I thought was a terrible mistake. He emphasized his status as a physician, that he was financially independent, had no felony charges, would not charge the estate for administration, and that he would be fair and fully comply with his grandmother's last wishes. Also, he did not have any liens on the estate.

6. After the judge heard both sides, he made a ruling to dismiss the temporary administrator and appoint my son as the independent executor of the estate. That act legally took the estate out of the State of Texas Administration and put it back into my family's hands, as my parents intended it to be.

7. The last step is to issue a **Letter of Testamentary**. Letters testamentary, sometimes referred to as letters of administration or letters of representation, are legal documents issued by a court to grant authority and designate an individual or executor to administer the estate of a deceased person. These letters are typically issued to the person named as the executor in the decedent's last will and testament, giving them the right to collect, manage, and distribute the assets of the estate according to the wishes outlined in the will. Letters testamentary provide the executor with the legal authority to handle various tasks related to the estate, such as paying debts, filing tax returns, managing assets, selling property, and distributing inheritance to beneficiaries. The issuance of these letters is an important step in the probate process, allowing the executor to act on behalf of the estate and carry out the necessary duties. More importantly, this act restored my mother's constitutional right to have her last

wishes complied with - a birthright of every U.S. citizen. The Texas Supreme Court upheld that right in their rulings in similar cases that I have highlighted earlier.

Lessons Learned!

1. The appellate court is a different entity with a whole new set of rules. Legal consultation is strongly recommended because of the complex rules and regulations.
2. Being highly organized is imperative. There was more paperwork to keep up with than at any other time of my life.
3. Again, I witnessed how the courts are inept in identifying and handling sociopathic, psychopathic, substance abusers, and otherwise very maladapted people and the devastating aftermath that is left in their wake.
4. Being forced to endure endless hours of insults and falsehoods directed at my child by bitter family members was incredibly painful. It is truly pathetic that they attempted to discredit my son solely because they themselves were inadequate and lacked the trust of our parents. The whole spectacle was a shameful display for

everyone involved, resulting in a pointless drain of money, time, and resources. The only ones who benefited were those profiting off the hours they billed.

5. The probate court needs to be overhauled, and I hope that this book will serve as an advocate for that cause. The biggest problem is the misalignment of incentives for the officers of the court to conduct themselves in a manner that is professional, ethical, and engenders public trust.

6. There does not appear to be a consistent mechanism in place to protect the vulnerable elderly from family members who will harm them out of their own desperation and ill will.

Actionable Steps

- Speak out against Elder Abuse, Estate Trafficking, and the weaponizing of the courts against innocent vulnerable citizens and the ones that are trying to protect them.
- Lobby to reform the broad judicial immunity clauses that allow judges too much discretion to violate people's constitutional rights.

- Put an estate plan together to protect yourself in your later years. Choose carefully the person that you want to look after your affairs if you are not able to.
- Consider having co-executors and two people who get along and love you unconditionally as your Power of Attorney. It's an extra layer of protection against relatives and probate court officials who will not have your best interest in mind.
- Don't give up! Go as far up the legal chain as you can. For me, this meant finding a balance between legacy and prosperity. I took the path of representing myself because I had an obligation to finish the job that I started—ensuring and restoring my parents' legacy, and I had an equal responsibility to myself and my family to not go bankrupt in the process. By remaining focused and dedicated to my goals, the path to finding solutions became unmistakably clear.

CHAPTER 9. REFLECTIONS AND DISCUSSION OF LESSONS LEARNED

Throughout this entire process, I have undergone a profound journey of self-discovery and witnessed the depth of love and gratitude within me. As I observed my own mother's world being turned upside down by her own family, I was filled with a sense of awe and admiration for her strength and resilience. The sadistic actions taken against my mother and the escalation of her persecution only fueled her determination to speak out about the rights she was being deprived of and the desire to maintain our unbreakable bond. Despite the challenging circumstances, she never wavered or allowed her spirit to be crushed. Her unwavering bravery, courage, and unyielding faith in God became a beacon of inspiration for me.

As I reflect on our journey together, I am humbled by the love and unwavering trust she had in me. Until her last breath, she made it known to anyone who would listen that I was her advocate and voice. This recognition fueled my own passion to carry forward our joint mission of raising awareness, promoting education, advocating for reforms within the guardianship and probate systems, and ensuring the protection of vulnerable individuals. Witnessing the resilience and determination of my mother has instilled within me a deeper sense of purpose. I am driven by her example to continue our fight for justice, striving to create a system that upholds the rights and dignity of individuals who find themselves entangled in abusive guardianships.

Our journey has taught me the significance of inner strength, the power of love, and the importance of unwavering faith in the face of adversity. It has propelled me to become an advocate, an educator, and a voice for those who cannot speak for themselves. The memory of my mother's courage and her unwavering trust in me serves as a constant reminder of the responsibility I have to fight for a more just and compassionate system. With a renewed sense of purpose, I am dedicated to raising awareness, effecting change in guardianship and probate processes, and preventing others from experiencing the injustices and traumas that afflicted my own family. By sharing our story, spreading awareness, and advocating for reforms, I hope to bring about a transformative impact and protect the rights and well-being of vulnerable individuals. In memory of my remarkable mother and with limitless gratitude for her love and trust, I will continue to channel the bravery, courage, and unyielding faith that she embodied.

In this book, ***Justice Served***, I have recounted my personal journey seeking justice in the face of filing a civil lawsuit against a judge. As the narrative reached its climax, I appealed the lawsuit all the way up to the 15th Circuit in New Orleans, presenting a substantial amount of evidence. I stopped short of the U.S. Supreme Court. Despite my efforts, the lawsuit was ultimately dismissed on the grounds of "judicial immunity." Regardless of the outcome, I had a major win because the lawsuit was the foundation of the successful recusal, reclaiming my mother's estate and honoring her last wishes.

I also won because, unbeknownst to me, the story of my fight to save my mother and the legal setbacks that I endured resonated with influential voters. Thus, the judge was not only unseated from presiding over my mother's case, but he lost his bid for re-election too. Lastly, I have won an initial bid to protect other families that are behind me by raising awareness. If this could happen to my mother, the most beautiful human being who was full of love and life, and to me, a physician, with a great career that I worked very hard for and was recently voted a Top Doc in the Maryland, DC, and Virginia area – it could happen to anyone!!

However, this is just the beginning of a war that has been long-standing and systemic. The dismissal of the lawsuit based on immunity raises urgent concerns about accountability and adherence to the rule of law. Immunity, a legal principle designed to protect public officials from personal liability while performing their duties, can sometimes shield individuals from consequences, even when there is evidence suggesting misconduct or wrongdoing. This global issue of judicial immunity can hinder the pursuit of justice, undermine trust in the legal system, and impede efforts to achieve true accountability. More importantly, abusive guardianships go undetected.

Reflections and Discussion of Lessons Learned

Abusive guardianships occur when appointed guardians or individuals entrusted with the care and protection of vulnerable adults exploit their positions for personal gain. They may mismanage finances, manipulate legal proceedings, isolate the elderly, or neglect their physical and emotional well-being. These cases involve violating the fundamental rights and dignity of elderly individuals, often leaving them financially devastated, socially isolated, and without recourse. The estimated cost of lost estates due to abusive guardianships is staggering. It is difficult to quantify precisely as cases often go unreported or undetected, but various reports and studies suggest that the financial losses resulting from abusive guardianships run into billions of dollars annually. These lost assets can include personal savings, homes, valuable possessions, and other financial investments that were intended to provide security and support in the elder's remaining years. The financial impact is not the only consequence; the emotional toll on the victims and their families is equally distressing, as is the loss of independence, dignity, and trust in the legal system.

Unholy Alliances

Abusive guardianships and probate courts pose significant challenges and present various problems that undermine the well-being and rights of vulnerable individuals. Here are some key observations:

1. **Overbroad Judicial Immunity:** Judicial immunity, intended to protect judges from personal liability while performing their duties, can sometimes be overbroad. This immunity has the unintended consequence of shielding judges from accountability even in cases of alleged misconduct or improper actions within guardianship and probate court proceedings. As a result, victims of abusive guardianships may face significant hurdles in seeking redress for any harm suffered.

2. **Misaligned Incentives:** The incentives within the guardianship system are not always aligned with the best interests of the vulnerable individuals involved. In some cases, financial profit becomes a motivating factor for certain participants, leading to conflicts of interest and potential exploitation. This misalignment may create an environment that prioritizes the preservation of financial

assets over the protection of an individual's rights and well-being.

3. **Formation of Alliances:** Disgruntled family members seeking financial gain might form alliances with attorneys involved in the guardianship process. Their shared goal is often to thwart the efforts of other family members advocating for the protection of their vulnerable loved ones. This alliance may resort to misinformation, lies, and malicious interference to block the rightful attempts to safeguard the interests of the vulnerable individual.

4. **Lack of Oversight and Accountability:** The guardianship and probate courts have limited oversight, which can contribute to potential abuses. The absence of comprehensive monitoring, periodic reviews, and transparent reporting requirements can create an environment where misconduct can go undetected or unaddressed. This lack of accountability can perpetuate a system that is vulnerable to abuses of power. These problems highlight the need for reforms within the guardianship and probate court systems to ensure that the

focus remains on the protection and welfare of vulnerable individuals.

Some Potential Solutions

- Implementing clearer guidelines and standards for judges, guardians, and attorneys involved in guardianship cases, promoting transparency, accountability, and ethical conduct.
- Subjecting guardianship proceedings to regular and independent audits to identify any irregularities or potential abuses.
- Establishing impartial oversight bodies or guardianship review panels to monitor guardianship cases, investigate complaints, and hold individuals who have engaged in improper actions accountable.
- Strengthening legal protections for family members seeking to advocate for the best interests of their vulnerable loved ones, ensuring their voices are heard and their efforts to protect are not unfairly hindered.

Addressing these problems requires public awareness, advocacy for policy changes, and legal reforms, which is the Call to Action that I concluded with. By shedding light on the shortcomings within abusive guardianships and probate courts, we can work towards a more equitable and protective system that truly serves the best interests of vulnerable individuals and their families.

Mental Health Issues

As previously stated, the courts face significant challenges when it comes to detecting family members with mental illness or substance use disorders who have ulterior motives to gain direct access to the victim's estate. These individuals may be driven by a range of negative emotions, including vindictiveness, jealousy, vengeance, entitlement, and financial desperation. The court system's limitations in identifying and addressing these complex situations can allow these individuals to exploit the vulnerabilities of the victim and manipulate legal processes for their own gain.

Some of the reasons for these challenges include:

- **Complexity of Mental Illness and Substance Use Disorders:** Mental health conditions and substance use disorders can be multifaceted and varied. Detecting these issues can be challenging, especially when individuals may hide their struggles or exhibit manipulative behaviors. The court system often lacks the necessary resources and expertise to thoroughly assess and diagnose mental health or substance-related problems.
- **Burden of Proof:** Properly identifying and addressing mental illness or substance use disorders requires substantial evidence and expert testimony. For the court to take action, it often relies on verifiable proof of the individual's impaired capacity or detrimental behavior. Obtaining such evidence can be difficult, particularly in cases where the individual is adept at manipulating or concealing their true intentions.
- **Limited Time and Resources:** Courts are often burdened with heavy caseloads, and judges may have limited time and resources to thoroughly investigate the complexities underlying family dynamics and individual motivations. In some instances, this can result in missed opportunities

to identify and address the underlying issues that are driving family members' harmful actions.

Addressing these challenges requires a multi-faceted approach:

- **Increased Mental Health and Substance Abuse Awareness:** Enhancing awareness and education among legal professionals, judges, and court personnel about the complexities of mental illness and substance use disorders is crucial. This can help improve their understanding of the potential motivations and behaviors of family members seeking to exploit vulnerable individuals.
- **Collaboration with Mental Health Professionals:** Foster collaboration between the legal system and mental health professionals. This collaboration can provide courts with access to expert evaluations, assessments, and treatment recommendations necessary to identify and address mental health or substance-related issues.
- **Strengthening Safeguard Measures:** Implement safeguards within the legal system to protect the rights and interests of vulnerable individuals. This could include requiring thorough psychological evaluations, appointing

independent advocates for the victim, or assigning a court-appointed guardian to oversee the circumstances and ensure the victim's well-being.

- **Legal Reforms:** Advocate for legal reforms that address issues concerning the protection of vulnerable individuals in guardianship and estate matters. These reforms may involve stricter oversight, mandatory reporting requirements, or enhanced protections for victims and their estates.

Recognizing the intersection of mental health, substance abuse, and exploitation within the legal system is crucial in safeguarding the rights and well-being of vulnerable individuals. Collaborative efforts, awareness, education, and policy changes can help improve the court's ability to detect and address the complex motivations of family members seeking to exploit vulnerable individuals for personal gain.

Reflections and Discussion of Lessons Learned

My Advice to Others Who May Find Themselves in a Similar Situation

In the face of daunting legal battles within the guardianship and probate court, it can be incredibly challenging to stand up for your rights and defend loved ones against abusive guardianships. However, it is crucial to remember that you have the power to make a difference and protect those who are vulnerable. Here are some encouraging points and strategies to consider:

- **Embrace Courage and Persistence:** Facing adversarial attorneys and disgruntled family members aligned against you can be intimidating. Many times I felt like David fighting Goliath. Remembering that David won helped a lot. Also, remember that standing up for what is right often requires courage and persistence. Stay determined and steadfast in your pursuit of justice, drawing strength from the knowledge that you are fighting for the well-being and rights of someone who needs your support and for others who will come behind you and be in the same situation.
- **Seek Expert Advice:** Engage the services of an experienced attorney who specializes in elder law and

guardianship matters. They can guide you through the complex legal landscape, help craft a strong legal strategy, and provide you with the necessary knowledge to navigate the specific rules, regulations, and codes of conduct applicable to your case. Their expertise will be invaluable in defending yourself and the victim you are trying to protect.

- **Document and Preserve Evidence:** Maintain meticulous records of all relevant documents, communications, and financial transactions related to the guardianship and probate court proceedings. This evidence can serve as a vital foundation for building your case, exposing any misconduct or breaches of regulations, and defending against false accusations. Ensure that you have a clear paper trail to support your claims.

- **Uphold Ethical and Legal Standards:** Know and abide by the ethical and legal standards applicable to your jurisdiction. Familiarize yourself with the relevant codes of conduct, estate laws, and regulations governing guardianships and probate court proceedings. By adhering to these standards, you not only protect yourself but also establish credibility and reinforce your commitment to upholding justice.

- **Seek Support and Allies:** Reach out to support groups, community organizations, and advocacy networks that specialize in elder rights or guardianship issues. These platforms can provide invaluable emotional support, guidance, and recommendations for legal resources. Surrounding yourself with a supportive community can bolster your strength and resilience throughout the process.

- **Educate Yourself and Raise Awareness:** Invest time in understanding the complexities of guardianship and probate court systems. Educate yourself on the rights and regulations that safeguard vulnerable individuals, and share this knowledge with others. By raising awareness about abusive guardianships and advocating for reform, you contribute to the greater movement for change and help prevent future injustices.

Remember, every case is unique, and legal battles can be complex. It is crucial to consult with an attorney who can provide personalized advice based on your specific circumstances. They can guide you on the applicable rules and regulations and help develop a robust legal strategy to protect yourself and the person you seek to defend. Stay resilient, determined, and committed to the pursuit of justice - together, we can challenge abusive guardianships and advocate for a more equitable and compassionate system.

CHAPTER 10. CONCLUSION AND CALL TO ACTION

My mother's case checks off all the boxes of being an abusive, financially exploitive, and defectively created guardianship. In my very humble opinion, this case meets the criteria for both elderly and estate trafficking that should be covered by the protections under RICO since it is intended to prevent and dismantle racketeering issues.

Beyond the specific case at hand, it is important to acknowledge the broader implications for society. In the realm of probate court and the treatment of the elderly and their estates. Judicial immunity can potentially facilitate the insidious practice of trafficking. Elderly trafficking involves various forms of exploitation, including financial abuse, neglect, or even physical and emotional manipulation of vulnerable individuals. Estate trafficking, on the other hand, occurs when individuals exploit their positions within probate court to improperly influence the distribution of assets, often to their personal benefit.

To combat these issues, the Racketeer Influenced and Corrupt Organizations (RICO) Act may be a relevant tool. RICO, a federal law originally designed to combat organized crime, can be applied to situations where individuals or organizations engage in a pattern of illegal activity connected to the abuse of power as can be seen within some probate courts. By utilizing RICO, prosecutors and advocates can potentially uncover underlying corruption, dismantle networks of exploitation, and hold those who perpetrate abuses within these systems, including the probate system, accountable. The aim of shedding light on the components of elderly trafficking, estate trafficking, and the potential application of RICO is to ignite a necessary dialogue on these grave matters.

Call to Action: Reforming the Guardianship and Probate System

We, as advocates for justice and fairness, are compelled to act and demand reforms within the guardianship and probate system. The flaws and injustices that have plagued this system for far too long cannot be ignored any longer. We must come together to effect significant change and ensure the protection of the vulnerable individuals who find themselves entangled in this flawed system.

Call to Action

Here is our call to action:

1. **Raise Awareness:** Spread awareness about the issues and challenges within the guardianship and probate system. Share personal stories, experiences, and the consequences that individuals and families have faced. Educate others about the need for reform and the urgency to address these systemic issues.

2. **Advocate for Legislative Reform:** Engage with lawmakers and advocate for legislative changes that promote transparency, accountability, and fairness within the guardianship and probate system. Push for laws that protect individuals from abusive practices, establish clear guidelines and standards, and hold guardians and professionals accountable for their actions.

3. **Promote Ethical Standards:** Advocate for the implementation of consistent and stringent ethical standards for guardians, attorneys, judges, and other professionals involved in guardianship and probate proceedings. Demand clear codes of conduct that prioritize the rights and well-being of vulnerable individuals, as well as measures to detect and address conflicts of interest.

4. **Strengthen Oversight and Accountability:** Push for increased oversight and monitoring mechanisms to detect and prevent abuses of power. Establish independent oversight bodies and regular audits to ensure compliance and proper evaluation of guardianship cases. Demand accountability for those who engage in misconduct or unethical behaviors.

5. **Enhance Access to Legal Aid and Representation:** Advocate for increased access to legal aid services for individuals involved in guardianship proceedings. Many vulnerable individuals and their families may lack the resources to afford legal representation. By expanding

Conclusion and Call to Action

legal aid availability, we can ensure fair and equal access to justice.

6. **Support Research and Data Collection:** Encourage research initiatives to collect comprehensive data on guardianship and probate cases, highlighting trends, abuses, and areas of improvement. This data can serve as an important tool to advocate for change and support evidence-based reforms.

7. **Engage Community Organizations:** Work closely with community organizations, nonprofits, and advocacy groups that focus on elder rights, guardianship reform, and legal system improvement. Collaborate to amplify the voices of those affected, leverage collective resources, and foster a stronger movement for change.

8. **Foster Collaboration and Interdisciplinary Dialogue:** Facilitate dialogue and collaboration among legal professionals, healthcare providers, social workers, psychologists, and other relevant stakeholders. Promote interdisciplinary approaches to address the complex challenges facing individuals within the guardianship and probate system.

We cannot stand by while vulnerable individuals and their families continue to suffer due to a system that is broken. Join me in raising our voices, demanding reform, and creating a robust guardianship and probate system that safeguards the rights, dignity, and well-being of those who need it most. Together, we can bring about meaningful change and ensure a more just and compassionate future.

As this chapter concludes, I hope ***Justice Served*** serves as a catalyst for change and fosters a renewed commitment to fairness, accountability, and the rule of law. Only by uniting in our efforts and advocating for reforms can we hope to rectify the injustices that currently plague our legal system and protect the rights and well-being of those most in need of our support and deserving of living the rest of their lives with dignity, security, and peace of mind.

DEFINITIONS, ROLES, AND RESPONSIBILITIES

Guardianship: A legal process in which a court appoints a guardian to make personal and/or financial decisions on behalf of an individual who is unable to make decisions due to incapacity, disability, or vulnerability.

Absolute Judicial Immunity: Absolute judicial immunity is a legal doctrine that protects judges from personal liability for monetary damages in civil court for acts they perform pursuant to their judicial function. Its purpose is to preserve the independence of the judiciary by ensuring that judges can make decisions without fear of personal repercussions.

In Texas, like most states, judges are generally granted absolute judicial immunity. This means that as long as they are acting within their judicial capacity, they cannot be sued for their decisions, even if those decisions are made maliciously or corruptly.

However, there are limitations to this immunity. Judges do not have immunity for actions that are taken outside of their judicial duties or when they act in the complete absence of all jurisdiction. In addition, while absolute judicial immunity protects judges from being personally sued for monetary damages, it does not protect them from criminal liability or from impeachment and removal from office.

It's important to note that complaints about a judge's conduct can still be made to the Texas State Commission on Judicial Conduct, which has the power to discipline judges for violations of judicial ethics rules.

Ward: The individual who is subject to guardianship and is considered legally incapacitated or vulnerable.

Probate Court: A specialized court that handles matters related to the distribution of estates, validation of wills, appointment of guardians, and resolution of disputes involving these matters.

Definitions, Roles, and Responsibilities

Incapacity: The state of being mentally, physically, or legally unable to make informed decisions or care for oneself.

Fiduciary: A fiduciary is a person or entity entrusted with managing property or other responsibilities. They have a legal duty to act in the best interest of the person they represent.

Power of Attorney (POA): A legal document that grants a designated person (the agent) the authority to act on behalf of another person (the principal) in financial, legal, or personal matters.

Advanced Healthcare Directive: A legal document that outlines an individual's wishes regarding medical treatments and end-of-life care in the event they become unable to make decisions.

Will: A legal document that expresses an individual's wishes regarding the distribution of their property, assets, and guardianship of minor children after their death.

Estate: The total value of a deceased person's property, assets, and financial holdings. It includes both tangible and intangible belongings.

Temporary Guardian: A temporary guardian in Texas has specific responsibilities under the law. As per the Texas Estates Code, a temporary guardian is appointed when there is substantial evidence that a person may be incapacitated, and the court has probable cause to believe so. These guardians are often appointed in an as-needed situation, usually immediately, to protect the ward.

The responsibilities of a temporary guardian can include:

- **Guardianship of the Person:** This involves taking care of the physical and personal needs of the ward. This could include decisions about medical care, housing, and day-to-day living.
- **Guardianship of the Estate:** A guardian of the estate has control over the ward's property and finances. They are responsible for managing the ward's assets and making financial decisions on their behalf.

- **Legal Obligations:** The temporary guardian must qualify in the same form and manner as required for a permanent guardian. This includes understanding and fulfilling all legal requirements and duties outlined in the Texas Estates Code.
- **Protection of the Ward:** Temporary guardianships are primarily appointed to protect the interests of the ward. This could involve ensuring their safety, protecting their rights, or providing care during a period of incapacity.

Guardian Ad Litem (GAL): A guardian ad litem (GAL) is a person the court appoints to investigate what solutions would be in the best interests of a child or individual in need. Here are some of the general roles and responsibilities:

- **Investigation:** The GAL investigates the facts of the case, reviews documents, and interviews people involved in the life of the child or incapacitated adult. This can include parents, caregivers, doctors, teachers, and the individual themselves.
- **Representation in Court:** The GAL represents the best interests of the child or individual during court

proceedings. They provide the court with a written report and make recommendations based on their investigation.

- **Monitoring:** After the court makes a decision, the GAL may be required to monitor the situation to ensure compliance with the court's orders and report back any issues.
- **Advocacy:** A GAL advocates for the individual's best interests, which may include ensuring they receive appropriate care, education, and services. They also ensure their rights are protected.
- **Confidentiality:** The GAL must maintain confidentiality and cannot disclose information about the case unless required by the court or law.
- **Impartiality:** The GAL should remain impartial throughout the process. They should not take sides but focus on what is best for the child or individual.

Attorney Ad Litem: An attorney ad litem (AAL) is a lawyer appointed by the court to represent and protect the legal rights and interests of a person during a particular lawsuit. This person could be a minor, an incapacitated adult, or someone who cannot represent themselves due to certain circumstances. Here are some of the roles and responsibilities of an attorney ad litem:

- **Representation:** The AAL represents their client in all proceedings related to the lawsuit. They have a duty to advocate for their client's best legal interests.
- **Investigation:** They are responsible for obtaining as much information as possible about the case to make informed recommendations and decisions. This can involve reviewing documents, interviewing relevant parties, and gathering evidence.
- **Counseling:** The AAL advises their client about their legal rights and options, potential outcomes of the case, and the legal process. They help their client understand and navigate the legal system.
- **Communication:** They maintain regular and open communication with their client to keep them informed about the progress of the case.
- **Confidentiality:** Just like any attorney-client relationship, the AAL has a duty to maintain confidentiality. They

cannot disclose information about the case unless required by law or court order.

- **Advocacy:** The AAL advocates for their client's wishes to the extent it is legally appropriate. They present arguments, file motions, and take other necessary actions to protect their client's rights and interests.
- **Reporting:** Depending on the jurisdiction, the AAL may need to provide the court with written reports about their findings and recommendations.
- **Impartiality:** While the AAL advocates for their client's interests, they should also remain impartial and not allow personal feelings to influence their professional duties.

REFERENCES

1. Guardianship

1. "Rights & Responsibilities - Guardianship" by Texas State Law Library.
2. "Powers and Duties of Guardian" by Riddle & Butts, LLP.
3. "Guardianship Responsibilities" by Texas Guardianship Association. https://www.texasguardianship.org/guardianship-responsibilities
4. "What are the Responsibilities of a Legal Guardian?" by Texas Trust Law. https://www.texastrustlaw.com/what-are-the-responsibilities-of-a-legal-guardian/
5. 3 Things to Know About Legal Guardianship in Texas" by Dallas Probate Law Firm. https://www.dallasprobatelawfirm.com/3-things-to-know-about-legal-guardianship-in-texas
6. "Frequently Asked Questions about Guardianship in Texas" by Keith Morris Attorney at Law. http://www.texas-probate-attorney.net/our-

services/guardianship-litigation-administration/guardianship-faqs/

7. "Duties and Responsibilities of a Guardian In Texas" by Law Office of Bryan Fagan.
   https://www.bryanfagan.com/blog/2023/september/duties-and-responsibilities-of-a-guardian-in-tex/

8. Guardianship Guide" by Texas Bar.
   https://www.texasbar.com/AM/Template.cfm?Section=Free_Legal_Information2&Template=/CM/ContentDisplay.cfm&ContentID=37357

9. Texas Guardianship.
   https://www.texasguardianship.org/guardianship-responsibilities/

10. Texas Estates Code Chapter 1251.
    https://statutes.capitol.texas.gov/Docs/ES/htm/ES.1251.htm

11. Texas Estates Code Chapter 1151.
    https://statutes.capitol.texas.gov/Docs/ES/htm/ES.1151.htm

References

12. Texas Young Lawyers Association.
    https://www.tyla.org/tyla/assets/File/AttorneyAdLitems Handbook.pdf

2. *Pro se* Litigation

1. Lucas County, Ohio - Step-By-Step Guide to Pro Se Litigation or How to Represent...
   https://co.lucas.oh.us/DocumentCenter/Home/View/8052
2. California Courts - Handling Cases Involving Self-Represented Litigants.
   https://www.courts.ca.gov/documents/benchguide_self_rep_litigants.pdf/
3. Wisconsin Courts - Pro Se: Meeting the challenge of self-represented litigants.
   https://www.wicourts.gov/publications/reports/docs/prosereport.pdf
4. U.S. Courts - Pro Se Centers Help Even the Odds for Litigants Without Lawyers.
   https://www.uscourts.gov/news/2015/08/20/pro-se-centers-help-even-odds-litigants-without-lawyers

5. The American Bar Association - The Proper Approach to Pro Se Litigants.
https://www.americanbar.org/groups/litigation/committees/pretrial-practice-discovery/practice/2020/proper-approach-to-pro-se-litigants/

3. The Texas Rules of Civil Procedure

The Texas Rules of Civil Procedure are a set of rules established by the Texas Supreme Court that govern the procedure in the state courts of Texas. They aim to obtain a just, fair, equitable, and impartial adjudication of the rights of litigants.

These rules cover various aspects of civil proceedings, including how depositions are obtained (Rule 201.1), practices in Justice Courts (Part V), special proceedings such as trespass to try title (Part VII, Rule 798), and more.

The Texas Rules of Civil Procedure can be accessed online from several sources, including:
1. The official website of the Texas Courts.

References

https://www.txcourts.gov/media/1446498/trcp-all-updated-with-amendments-effective-may-1-2020.pdf

2. State Law Library of Texas.
   https://www.sll.texas.gov/the-courts/texas-court-rules/
3. Casetext. https://casetext.com/rule/texas-court-rules/texas-rules-of-civil-procedure
4. South Texas College of Law Houston.
   https://www.stcl.edu/library/special-collections/texas-rules/)
5. Westlaw.
   https://today.westlaw.com/Document/Ic1261b6a55ea11ebbea4f0dc9fb6957

Filing a Lawsuit in Federal Court

Filing a lawsuit in federal court in Texas involves several steps. Please note that this information is a general overview and may not cover all aspects of your situation. Always consult with a legal professional for advice specific to your case.

- **Ensure You Have a Valid Claim:** Before you begin, make sure that you have a valid and viable legal claim that falls under federal jurisdiction. This could be a matter involving federal law or a dispute between residents of different states where the amount in dispute exceeds $75,000[1].

- **Prepare Your Complaint:** The complaint is the document that starts your lawsuit. It should include a statement of the facts constituting your claim, the legal basis for the court's jurisdiction, and the relief you are seeking[2].

- **File Your Complaint:** If you are filing on paper, an original plus one copy is required. The Clerk's Office will retain the original for the case file and send a copy to the judge[3]. Alternatively, you may be able to file electronically[4].

- **Pay the Filing Fee:** There is a fee associated with filing a lawsuit in federal court. If you can't afford the fee, you can apply for a fee waiver.

- **Serve the Defendant:** After you file your complaint, you must serve a copy of it along with a summons to appear in court to the defendant. This is usually done by a process server or law enforcement officer.

- **Follow Court Procedures:** Once your case is underway, you'll need to follow all procedural rules, including

References

deadlines for filing documents, participating in discovery, and attending court hearings.

References are as follows:
1. LegalMatch. https://www.legalmatch.com/law-library/article/how-to-sue-in-texas.html
2. Federal Bar Association Pro Se Handbook. https://www.fedbar.org/wp-content/uploads/2019/12/Pro-Se-Handbook-APPROVED-v2019-2.pdf
3. U.S. District Court for the Northern District of Texas. https://www.txnd.uscourts.gov/faq/filing
4. Texas Courts eFiling Guide. https://www.txcourts.gov/media/1442179/tyla-guide-how-to-efile-documents.pdf

(**Note:** When following any of the legal procedures presented in this section, please consult an attorney or certified legal advisor to evaluate the credibility, suitability, and legality of such steps.)

4. Appeals

Filing an appeal in Texas probate court involves several important steps. It's essential to follow these steps carefully and within the specified time frames, as failure to do so can result in your appeal being dismissed. Here are the basic steps for filing an appeal:

- **Determine if You Can Appeal:** Not all probate court decisions can be appealed. Generally, you can appeal a final judgment of the probate court.
- **File a Notice of Appeal:** The first step in the appeals process is to file a notice of appeal with the trial court clerk. This notice must be filed within 30 days of the judgment[3].
- **Prepare the Appellate Record:** The appellate record typically includes the trial court clerk's record and, if necessary, a reporter's record (a transcription of court proceedings). For an electronic clerk's record, unless the clerk receives permission from the appellate court to file the record in paper form, the clerk must file the record electronically[1].

References

- **File a Docketing Statement:** Once the trial court clerk has assigned the appeal to the First Court, the appellant must file a docketing statement with the clerk[4].
- **Submit Briefs:** After the appellate record is complete, you'll have to submit a brief outlining your arguments for why the trial court's decision should be reversed or modified.
- **Oral Argument:** In some cases, the appellate court may schedule an oral argument, where each side has a chance to present their case directly to the judges.
- **Wait for Decision:** After reviewing the briefs and hearing oral arguments (if applicable), the appellate court will issue a decision.

Please note that the deadline to appeal a Texas probate court order or judgment can be very short, sometimes as little as 20 days after entry of the judgment[5]. Also, remember that the process can be complicated and usually requires a lawyer's assistance.

References are as follows:

1. Texas Rules of Appellate Procedure. https://www.txcourts.gov/media/1437631/texas-rules-of-appellate-procedure-updated-with-amendments-effective-2117-with-appendices.pdf
2. Texas Inheritance Issues. https://www.texasinheritance.com/time-limits-for-appealing-a-will-contest-after-trial
3. DFW Probate Law. https://dfw-probate-law.com/does-a-probate-courts-order-have-to-be-final-to-be-appealable
4. First Court of Appeals - 1st COA. https://www.txcourts.gov/1stcoa/practice-before-the-court/forms
5. Probate Stars. https://probatestars.com/can-you-appeal-a-texas-probate-court-ruling/

(**Note:** When following any of the legal procedures presented in this section, please consult an attorney or certified legal advisor to evaluate the credibility, suitability, and legality of such steps.)

5. Filing a Complaint Against the Judge

If you wish to file a complaint against a probate judge in Texas, you can do so through the State Commission on Judicial Conduct. The process involves the following steps:

- **Download the Complaint Form:** You can find the form on the State Commission on Judicial Conduct's website. If you're unable to download the form, you can request one by emailing information@scjc.texas.gov or calling (512) 463-5533[1].

- **Fill Out the Form:** Complete the form with as much detail as possible. Your complaint should clearly state what you believe the judge did that may be misconduct, along with sufficient facts to describe what happened.

- **Submit the Form:** Once completed, submit your complaint. If you're filing a complaint about more than one judge, you should use a separate form for each judge[3].

- **Follow-Up:** After submitting your complaint, you may need to follow up with the commission. You can do this by writing to compliancedepartment@txcourts.gov, and make sure to reference your complaint currently before the Commission, including the Case Number (if applicable).

Please note that complaints should be submitted in writing. It's also important to know that the Commission does not have the authority to change a judge's decision or ruling - it only has the power to discipline judges for violations of judicial conduct.

References are as follows:
1. State Commission on Judicial Conduct – FAQ. https://www.scjc.texas.gov/faq
2. Texas Judicial Ethics Complaints.

    https://www.law.uh.edu/libraries/ethics/judicial/complaints/index.html
3. State Commission on Judicial Conduct. https://www.scjc.texas.gov/
4. TJB | JBCC | Compliance. https://www.txcourts.gov/jbcc/compliance/

(**Note:** When following any of the legal procedures presented in this section, please consult an attorney or certified legal advisor to evaluate the credibility, suitability, and legality of such steps.)

6. Filing a Complaint Against a Court-Appointed Attorney

If you would like to file a complaint against a court-appointed probate attorney in Texas, here are the steps you need to follow:

- **Obtain the Grievance Form:** You can find the grievance form on the State Bar of Texas's website. Alternatively, you can request a form by calling 1-800-932-1900[2].
- **Complete the Grievance Form:** In this form, you should provide as much detail as possible about the nature of your complaint. Include information about yourself, the attorney you're complaining about, and a comprehensive description of the misconduct.
- **Submit Your Complaint:** With the completed form, send it to the General Counsel's local office nearest to you[2]. If you're unsure where to send your form, you can call 1-800-932-1900 for guidance[2].

- **Wait for Investigation:** Once your complaint has been submitted, it will be reviewed by the Texas Office of Chief Disciplinary Counsel (CDC), which investigates allegations of professional misconduct[1].
- **Possible Disciplinary Action:** If the CDC investigation finds that the attorney engaged in professional misconduct, they could face disciplinary action, which might range from public reprimands to disbarment.

Please bear in mind that filing a complaint against an attorney is a serious matter and should only be done based on factual instances of misconduct. It's also important to understand that filing a complaint won't alter the outcome of your case. If you're dissatisfied with your court-appointed attorney because you believe their representation was ineffective, you may want to consult with another lawyer about possible remedies.

(**Note:** When following any of the legal procedures presented in this section, please consult an attorney or certified legal advisor to evaluate the credibility, suitability, and legality of such steps.)

References are as follows:
1. State Bar of Texas. https://cdc.texasbar.com/
2. Texas Attorney Ethics Complaints. https://www.law.uh.edu/libraries/ethics/attydiscipline/howfile.html

7. Removal or Recusal of a Judge

The recusal or disqualification of a judge in Texas is governed by several laws and rules including:

- **Texas Rules of Civil Procedure (Part II, Rule 18a & 18b):** These rules detail the process for requesting the recusal or disqualification of a judge. A judge's rulings may not be the sole basis for a motion to recuse or disqualify the judge. But when one or more sufficient other bases are present, a party can file a motion for recusal.
- **Texas Constitution and Code of Criminal Procedure (Article 30.01):** The grounds for disqualification are set out in these documents. No judge or justice of the peace

shall sit in any case where they may be the party injured, or where they have been of counsel for the State.
- **Texas Government Code (Section 25.00255):** This code section provides additional rules for the recusal or disqualification of a judge.
- **Texas Code of Judicial Conduct:** This code establishes the ethical standards for the conduct of judges, including situations where recusal or disqualification would be appropriate.

It's important to note that while these rules establish the legal framework for recusal or disqualification, the actual decision to recuse often depends on the specific circumstances of the case and the discretion of the judge. Always consult with a legal professional for advice related to a specific situation or case.

References are as follows:
- Rule 18a - Recusal and Disqualification of Judges. https://casetext.com/rule/texas-court-rules/texas-rules-of-civil-procedure/part-ii-rules-of-practice-in-district-and-

county-courts/section-1-general-rules/rule-18a-recusal-and-disqualification-of-judges
- Rule 18b - Grounds for Recusal and Disqualification of Judges. https://casetext.com/rule/texas-court-rules/texas-rules-of-civil-procedure/part-ii-rules-of-practice-in-district-and-county-courts/section-1-general-rules/rule-18b-grounds-for-recusal-and-disqualification-of-judges
- Code of Criminal Procedure Chapter 30. https://statutes.capitol.texas.gov/Docs/CR/htm/CR.30.htm
- Texas Government Code Section 25.00255. https://law.justia.com/codes/texas/2021/government-code/title-2/subtitle-a/chapter-25/subchapter-b/section-25-00255/
- Texas Code of Judicial Conduct. https://www.txcourts.gov/media/1457109/texas-code-of-judicial-conduct.pdf

(**Note:** When following any of the legal procedures presented in this section, please consult an attorney or certified legal advisor to evaluate the credibility, suitability, and legality of such steps.)

8. Resources

Here are some organizations that provide free or low-cost legal assistance, including to *pro se*:

- **Free Legal Answers:** An online *pro bono* program that matches low-income clients with volunteer lawyers who agree to provide brief answers online for free. https://www.americanbar.org/groups/legal_services/flh-home/flh-free-legal-help

- **List of *Pro Bono* Legal Service Providers:** This list is provided to individuals in immigration proceedings and contains information on non-profit organizations and attorneys who have committed to providing *pro bono* legal services. https://www.justice.gov/eoir/list-pro-bono-legal-service-providers.

- **Legal Aid Offices:** Not-for-profit agencies that provide free legal help to people who cannot afford to hire a lawyer. https://www.lawhelp.org/resource/legal-aid-and-other-low-cost-legal-help

References

- **Upsolve - Texas Bankruptcy:** A legal aid non-profit organization that provides legal information and assistance. https://www.tarrantcountytx.gov/en/law-library/free-low-cost-legal-assistance.html.
- **Florida Law Help, Free Legal Answers, Pro Se Handbook and *Pro Bono* Resources for Appeals, The Florida Bar, Local Bar Association's *Pro Bono* Resources:** These are various resources available in Florida offering free and low-cost legal aid. https://help.flcourts.gov/Legal-Services-Resources
- **Gulf Coast Legal Services:** Provides free legal assistance in areas such as foreclosure, elder law, and immigration. https://www.hillsbar.com/page/ProBonoAid
- **Utah Legal Clinics:** Some Utah organizations provide legal services for free, many of these organizations look at a person's income to determine whether they qualify for those services. https://www.utcourts.gov/en/legal-help/legal-help/finding-legal-help/legal-clinics/organizations.html/

Please remember to verify the eligibility criteria and services offered by each resource, as they may vary.

Resources on Guardianship and Probate Court Proceedings

- **Legal Information Institute - Cornell University Law School:** This resource provides a broad overview of guardianship and probate laws, as well as related topics such as estate planning and elder law. https://www.law.cornell.edu/wex/probate
- FindLaw's Estate Planning section includes a wealth of information on guardianship and probate, including detailed articles, legal forms, and a directory of estate planning lawyers.
  https://estate.findlaw.com/
- **National Guardianship Association:** The NGA provides educational resources and advocacy for guardianship professionals. Their website includes a resource center with publications, webinars, and other tools for guardians. https://www.guardianship.org/

Remember, while these resources provide valuable information, they are not a substitute for legal advice from a qualified attorney.

Organizations that Provide Legal Aid or Pro Se Support

- **American Bar Association (ABA):** The ABA provides a range of resources for those in need of legal aid, including a directory of *pro bono* programs and information about federally funded legal services. https://www.americanbar.org/groups/legal_services/flh-home/flh-free-legal-help/
- **LawHelp.org:** This not-for-profit agency provides free legal help to those who qualify. They also offer online *pro bono* programs. https://www.lawhelp.org/resource/legal-aid-and-other-low-cost-legal-help
- **USA.gov Legal Aid:** This government resource provides information about programs and organizations that offer free legal advice and may help individuals find a free or low-cost attorney. https://www.usa.gov/legal-aid

- **Justice Power's *Pro Se* Legal Clinics:** These clinics help immigrants understand and use available legal and non-legal resources to advocate for themselves https://www.justicepower.org/pro-se-legal-clinics/
- **Legal Services Corporation (LSC):** Established by Congress in 1974, the LSC provides financial support for civil legal aid to low-income Americans. https://www.lsc.gov/about-lsc/what-legal-aid/i-need-legal-help
- ***Pro Bono* Legal Service Providers:** The Department of Justice maintains a list of non-profit organizations and attorneys committed to providing *pro bono* legal services.
- https://www.justice.gov/eoir/list-pro-bono-legal-service-providers
- **St. Louis Bankruptcy *Pro Se* Assistance Program:** This program offers assistance to individuals representing themselves in bankruptcy cases. https://www.moed.uscourts.gov/pro-se-assistance-program

Remember, while these resources can provide valuable help, they are not a substitute for legal advice from a qualified attorney.

9. Further Reading and Research on Guardianship and Probate-Related Topics

i. Books:

1. *Guardianship, Conservatorship, and the Law* by Margaret C. Jasper.
2. *The Guardianship Book for California: How to Become a Child's Legal Guardian* by David Brown and Emily Doskow.
3. *Probate Wars of the Rich & Famous: An Insider's Guide to Estate Planning and Probate Litigation* by Russell J. Fishkind.
4. *Guardianships and the Elderly: The Perfect Crime* by Dr. Sam Sugar.

ii. Websites and Organizations:

- **National Guardianship Association (NGA):** Website:

htpps://www.guardianship.org

- **American Bar Association - Commission on Law and Aging:**

  htpps://www.americanbar.org/groups/law_aging

- **Justice in Aging:**

  www.justiceinaging.org/issues/guardianship

iii. Scholarly Articles and Reports:

- "Guardianships: Cases of Financial Exploitation, Neglect, and Abuse of Seniors" - Staff Report, U.S. Senate Special Committee on Aging (2018)
- "Guardianships: State Efforts to Protect Older Adults from Unnecessary Guardianships and to Facilitate Guardianship Termination" - U.S. Government Accountability Office (GAO) Report (2016)
- "Guardianship Practice: Exploring the Impact of State Variation on Older Adults" - Article by Jonathan D. Lauer and Robyn M. Powell published in the Journal of Elder Policy (2019)

References

- "Guardianship and Conservatorship: A Guide to Protecting the Elderly and Disabled" - Article by W. Mitten Brown published in the Journal of Financial Planning (2013)
- "It's not just Britney Spears: 1.3M Americans are under conservatorships. Activists want reform"- Article by Marc Ramirez and Romina Ruiz-Goiriena published in

  USA TODAY (2021) Sheila Owens-Collins, MD (current author) is profiled.

Please note that the availability of some resources may vary depending on your location and current publications. It is always advisable to stay updated with recent publications, reports, legal developments, and local resources specific to your jurisdiction. Additionally, consulting legal professionals, academic databases, and local legal aid organizations can also provide valuable insights and resources for further research into guardianship and probate matters.